The Use of Athletic Metaphors in the Biblical Homilies of St. John Chrysostom

A DISSERTATION

FACULTY OF PRINCETON UNIVERSITY
IN CANDIDACY FOR THE DEGREE
OF DOCTOR OF PHILOSOPHY

BY

JOHN ALEXANDER SAWHILL

*Professor of Classical Languages in
The State Teachers College at
Harrisonburg, Virginia*

I0153066

WIPF & STOCK · Eugene, Oregon

Wipf and Stock Publishers
199 W 8th Ave, Suite 3
Eugene, OR 97401

The Use of Athletic Metaphors in the Biblical Homilies of St. John Chrysostom
By Sawhill, John Alexander
Softcover ISBN-13: 978-1-7252-8837-9
Hardcover ISBN-13: 978-1-7252-8839-3
eBook ISBN-13: 978-1-7252-8838-6
Publication date 9/25/2020
Previously published by Princeton University Press, 1928

This edition is a scanned facsimile of the original edition published in 1928.

VXORI PARENTIBVSQVE DILECTISSIMIS

PREFACE

In presenting this dissertation I wish to express my gratitude and appreciation for aid of many kinds to Dean Andrew F. West, at whose suggestion this study was undertaken, and under whose direction it was written. I desire to thank Professor Edward Capps for many helpful suggestions made in reading the manuscript. I wish also to acknowledge my indebtedness to Professor P. R. Coleman-Norton for invaluable criticism and assistance in preparing the manuscript for the press and in reading the proof.

J. A. S.

Classical Seminary,
   Princeton University,
     July 22, 1927.

TABLE OF CONTENTS

	Page
Preface	5
Introduction	9
Part I. The Training for the Contest	10
Part II. The Contest	28
1. Regulations of the Games and Functions of the Presiding Official	29
2. Running	35
3. Wrestling	47
4. Boxing	65
5. Chariot-Racing	73
6. The Contest in General	78
Part III. The Prizes	90
Conclusion	110
Index of Athletic Terms	112

INTRODUCTION

The chief purpose of this study is to construct a logical classification of the athletic metaphors occurring in the Biblical Homilies of St. John Chrysostom (c. 347–407), whose use of athletic allusions is the most complete and illuminating of all early Greek Christian writers. Since all his athletic references concern Christian living and conduct of life, they may in general come under the title of *The Christian Athletic Contest*. This subject seems to divide itself naturally into three principal parts: first, the training for the contest; second, the contest proper; and third, the prizes obtained by the victorious Christian Athlete. Each part will be treated in such a way that each specific reference will fall into what seems to be its natural class.

The citations from St. Chrysostom's works refer to their edition by J. P. Migne in Vols. XLVII–LXIV of his *Patrologia Graeca* (Paris, 1859–1863). Cited thus: 55, 674, 21 means volume 55, column 674, line 21. The translations are based for the most part on the treatises of St. Chrysostom contained in Vols. IX–XIV of *A Select Library of the Nicene and Post-Nicene Fathers of the Christian Church* (edited by P. Schaff, New York, 1888–1893), with such changes as are, in my opinion, necessary for the expression of the full force of certain Greek words.

In a few instances illustrations are incorporated from treatises other than the Biblical Homilies for the purpose of presenting a better picture of the Contest.

PART I. THE TRAINING FOR THE CONTEST

For this part three main categories have been chosen: first, those who have special need of training; second, the various means of training; and third, the method of training. At times the second and third categories may seem to be a distinction without a difference. However, it is hoped that in the main a reasonable distinction may be apparent.

1. THOSE IN NEED OF TRAINING

There are two instances mentioned of those who stand in special need of training. The first concerns the Preacher. 48, 674, 51: "Since preaching comes not by nature, but by study, suppose that a man reaches a high standard of it,—this will then forsake him, if he does not cultivate his power by constant application and exercise (γυμνασίᾳ)."

The second deals with the Church, which must be kept in an athletic condition by its spiritual overseers. 48, 665, 13: "The Church of Christ, according to St. Paul, is Christ's Body [Col. I, 18], and he who is intrusted with its care ought to train it (ἐξασκεῖν) to a state of health and unspeakable beauty and to look everywhere, lest any spot or wrinkle or other like blemish should mar its vigor and comeliness. . . . If they who are ambitious of reaching an athletic condition of body need the help of physicians and trainers (παιδο-τριβῶν) and exact diet and constant exercise (ἀσκήσεως) and a thousand other rules (for the omission of the merest trifle upsets and spoils the whole), how shall they to whose lot falls the care of the body, which has its conflict (ἄθλησιν) not against flesh and blood, but against powers unseen, be able to keep it sound and healthy, unless they far surpass ordinary human virtue and are versed in all healing proper for the soul?"

2. MEANS OF TRAINING

There are several means of training. Three important institutions, the Church, the Monastery and the Home, contribute to this purpose. 61, 510, 19: "The Church may be justly called a training-course for that race (γυμνάσιον δρόμων) which leads to heaven."

The Monastery is a gymnasium for youth. 47, 380, 16: "Let us not be distressed or grieved, if our sons must pass ten or twenty years in a monastery. For the longer the training is in the gymnasium, so much greater will be the strength which they will acquire."

10

Stagirius, who is in conflict with the demon, is reminded how powerful his monastic training had made him before he entered the stadium. 47, 447, 34: "God did not call you to this contest of wrestling (πάλην) at once, when you entered upon the life of a monk, but allowed you first to be trained (ἐγγυμνασθῆναι) and remain a long time; and then, when you were made very powerful, He dragged you to this stadium (στάδιον) full of toils. . . . God let this demon upon you that you might contend (ἀγωνίσασθαι) nobly and conquer brilliantly and put on the crown of endurance."

The third institution for training is the Home. This is a *palaestra* for virtue, where, by having conquered many vices, one will have attained such perfect skill that one will be able to conquer all abroad. 57, 201, 11: "Let us learn first not to swear,[1] not to forswear ourselves, not to speak evil. Then let us learn not to envy, not to lust, not to be gluttonous, not drunken, not fierce, not slothful, so that from these we may pass on again to the things of the Spirit. And all these let us exercise (γυμνάζωμεν) in our home, with our friends, with our wife, with our children. And, for the present, let us begin with the things that come first and are easier: as, for instance, with not swearing. . . . Let your home be a sort of lists (ἀγών), a place of exercise (παλαίστρα) for virtue, that, having trained yourself (γυμνασάμενος) well there, you may with entire skill encounter all abroad. Do this with respect to vainglory also. For if you train yourself not to be vainglorious in company of your wife and your servants, you will not ever afterward be easily caught by this passion with regard to any one else. . . . And with respect to the other passions too, let us do this self-same thing, exercising ourselves (γυμναζόμενοι) against them at home and anointing ourselves (ἀλειφόμενοι) every day. Let each one, on returning home [from church], call his own wife and tell her these things and take her to help him; and from this day let him enter into that noble school of exercise (καλὴν παλαίστραν), using for oil (ἐλαίῳ) the supply of the Spirit. And though you fall once, twice, many times, in your training (γυμναζόμενος), despair not, but stand again and wrestle; and do not quit, until you have bound on you the glorious crown of triumph over the devil."

[1]Also in 60, 84, 39 refraining from swearing is a means of training and is considered sufficient to make a way for all virtue to enter. "Let all men see that of those who assemble in this Church not one is a swearer. . . . By our mouth and tongue let us be known, even as those who speak Greek are distinguished from barbarians. . . . If any one bids you swear, tell him, 'Christ has spoken, and I do not swear.' This is enough to make a way for all virtue to enter. . . . It is a training-school for piety (παλαίστρα τῆς εὐσεβείας)."

In the home a talkative wife may be a training-school and a helpful exercise. 60, 126, 19: "Nothing is more base or disgraceful or hurtful than passion. Men should not only be gentle among themselves, but they should also bear it, if their wives are talkative. Let your wife be to you a school for training and exercise (παλαίστρα καὶ γυμνάσιον). For how can it be but absurd to submit to exercises (γυμνάσια) which yield no profit, where we afflict the body, but not to practise exercises at home, which, even before the contest (ἀγώνων), present to us a crown?"

A comment on the most famous of Greek philosophers in dealing with a contentious wife is elicited by I Cor. XI, 16: "But if any man seemeth to be contentious, we have no such custom, neither the churches of God." 61, 224, 3: "It is said, for instance, that one of the heathen (τῶν ἔξωθεν)[1] philosophers, who had a bad wife, a trifler and a brawler, when asked why, having such an one, he endured her, replied that he might have in his house a school and training-place (γυμνάσιον καὶ παλαίστραν) of philosophy. 'For I shall be to all the rest meeker,' said he, 'being here disciplined every day.'"

The home should naturally be the proper training-place for the children who are reared in it. 62, 546, 41: "Let us train youth in chastity, for there is the very bane of youth. For this many struggles (ἀγώνων), much attention will be necessary. Let us take wives for them early, so that their brides may receive their bodies pure and unpolluted, so that their loves will be more ardent. . . . Garlands are wont to be worn on the heads of bridegrooms, as a symbol of victory, betokening that they approach the marriage-bed unconquered (μὴ κατηγωνίσθησαν) by pleasure." Ib. 548, 10: "Daughters should go from their father's house to marriage, as combatants—athletes (ἀθλητήν)—from the school of exercise(ἐκ παλαίστρας), furnished with all necessary knowledge(πᾶσαν δι' ἀκριβείας ἔχουσαν τὴν ἐπιστήμην)." There is this difference, however, in the case of the bride. She has been reared in the privacy of her father's house; whereas the palaestra is a public place, where one may be seen by all and where there is no privacy. Ib. 387, 14: "She comes forth at least from the nurse's arm, and not from the palaestra."

Poverty as a means of training is of no mean importance. 58, 791, 21: "It is a wrestling-ground (παλαίστρα) and school of exercise to learn self-command (γυμνάσιον φιλοσοφίας),[2] an imitation

---

[1] "Of those without;" a common ecclesiastical expression denoting those without the pale of the Church.

[2] St. Chrysostom frequently uses φιλοσοφία in the sense of Christian training, religious contemplation, moral discipline, and the monastic form of life. In 61, 588, 38 he exhorts men "to be noble and champions (ἀθληταί) of philosophy."

of the life of angels." God purposely did not make money common. 49, 43, 22: "And wherefore, one may say, is it that the greater and more necessary blessings and those which maintain our life God has made common; but the smaller and less valuable (I speak of money) are not thus common? Why?—in order that our life may be disciplined (συγκροτῆται) and that we may have a training-ground (σκάμματα) for virtue."

Closely allied with the idea of poverty is that of too much money, which fetters us in our wrestling with incorporeal powers. This point is considered in the comment on I Cor. IV, 16: "I beseech you therefore, be ye imitators of me." Here St. Chrysostom quotes I Cor. IX, 27: "... I buffet my body ...." and adds (61, 112, 45): "If we exercise ourselves, when we enter into the contest (ἀγῶνα), we shall be crowned; and, though there is no persecution before us, we shall receive for these things many prizes (βραβεῖα). How are we to overcome the incorporeal powers with which we wrestle? For if in wrestling with men one must be temperate in diet, much more with evil spirits. We must do away with not only fullness of flesh, but also the wealth with which we are bound down, in order that we may overcome our antagonists (ἀντιπάλων)."

St. Chrysostom in training the women of his congregation, like St. Paul, forbids the wearing of jewelry. 62, 350, 29: "If you women continue to act thus, I will not suffer it or receive you or permit you to pass across this threshold. For what need have I of a crowd of distempered (νοσούντων) people? And in my training (παιδοτριβῶν) of you, what if I forbid not what is excessive? And yet Paul forbade both gold and pearls [I Tim. II, 9]. We are mocked by the Greeks; our religion appears a fable."

Cares, affliction, defeat and chastisement are also means of training. 60, 378, 21: "A man without cares would soon revel in gluttony. But, as it is, cares and anxieties are an exercise (γυμνάσιον)." On II Cor. XII, 10: "... I take pleasure in ... distresses, for Christ's sake. . ." St. Chrysostom says (61, 579, 43): "Affliction rends away pride and anoints (ἀλείφει) to patience."

Chastisement is profitable in toning the condition of the soul, so that it may participate in holiness. Commenting on Heb. XII, 10: "... he [chastens us] for our profit, that we may be partakers of his holiness," St. Chrysostom says (63, 206, 55): "And that this is true appears from the fact that women raised in the country are stronger than citizens of towns; and they can overcome many such in wrestling (καταπαλαίσαιεν). For when the body becomes more effeminate, of necessity the soul also shares the mischief, since, for the most part, its energies are affected in accordance with the body."

That chastisement makes for invincibility in contests is also elaborated in the comment on Heb. XII, 11: ". . . chastening . . . afterward . . . yieldeth peaceable fruit unto them that have been exercised (γεγυμνασμένοις) thereby, even the fruit of righteousness." 63, 209, 29: "This means to those who have endured for a long while and have been patient. And he [St. Paul] uses an auspicious expression. So then, chastisement is exercise (γυμνασία), making the athlete strong and invincible in his combats (ἀκαταγώνιστον ἐν τοῖς ἀγῶσι)."

Continual hearing of the Scriptures exercises the senses of the soul. Heb. V, 14: "But solid food is for fullgrown men, even those who by reason of use have their senses exercised (γεγυμνασμένα) to discern good and evil." 63, 73, 31: "The senses of the soul become exercised (γεγυμνασμένα) by continual hearing, by experience of the Scriptures. . . . Even if you do not comprehend to-day, you shall comprehend to-morrow."

There is a special kind of training in the case of Adam and Eve (53, 133, 41), where eating of the fruit of the forbidden tree (thus causing them to know good and evil) may be called a training (γυμνασία) of obedience and disobedience.

Showing sympathy to animals is a means of training for human kindness, the idea being taken from Prov. XII, 10: "A righteous man regardeth the life of his beast. . . ." 64, 692, 27: "The training-place (γυμνάσιον) for human kindness is exhibited in showing sympathy to those animals which do not exercise reason. One who pities these will much more do so in the case of a brother. . . . There is need of showing much human kindness, in order that we may be trained (ἐγγυμναζώμεθα) in respect to those of our own race."

Life has many things to exercise us, so that we need not resort to the sand-bags of the boxers. Heb. X, 24 suggests some of these means: "and let us consider one another to provoke unto love good works." 63, 142, 37: "If we love our enemies, we are doing good to ourselves; for God appoints the prize (ἔπαθλον) for us. Even for his wickedness you ought to feel grateful to him; for if he had not been exceedingly evil, your reward would not have been exceedingly increased. Take away the adversary (ἀνταγωνιστήν), and you take away the opportunity for the crowns. Do you not see the athletes (ἀθλητάς),[1] how they exercise (γυμνάζονται), when they have filled

---

[1]Savile conjectures τοὺς πύκτας.

the bags (θυλάκους) with sand? Life is full of things that exercise (τῶν γυμναζόντων) you and make you strong."

3. METHOD OF TRAINING

The Christian Athlete must learn to keep his body always in a fit condition and to be like St. Paul, who ever wished to hold himself qualified for the contest in which he was engaged. St. Chrysostom refers more than once to I Cor. IX, 27: "but I buffet (ὑπωπιάζω)[1] my body, and bring it into bondage: lest by any means, after that I have preached to others, I myself should be rejected[2] (ἀδόκιμος)." 61, 190, 24: "For do not, I pray you, suppose that by taking things easily I arrive at this desirable result. For it is a race (δρόμος) and a manifold struggle (παγκράτιον) and a tyrannical nature continually rising against me and seeking to free itself. But I bear not with it, but keep it down and bring it into subjection with many struggles. Now this he [St. Paul] says, so that none may despairingly withdraw from the conflicts (ἀγώνων) in behalf of virtue, because the undertaking is laborious. He said not, 'I kill' or 'I punish,' for the flesh must not be hated, but 'I buffet and bring into bondage,' which is the part of a gymnastic master (παιδοτρίβου), not of an adversary."

In commenting on II Tim. II, 5 St. Chrysostom discusses contending lawfully. 62, 619, 54: "What is meant by 'lawfully'? It is not enough that he enters the lists (ἀγῶνα), that he is anointed and even engages (συμπλακῇ), unless he complies with all the laws of exercise (ἀθλήσεως), with respect to diet (σιτίων), to temperance, to sobriety and to all the rules of the wrestling-school (παλαίστρᾳ); unless, in short, he goes through all that is befitting a wrestler (ἀθληταῖς), he is not crowned. Observe the wisdom of Paul. He mentions wrestling (ἀθλήσεως) to prepare him [St. Timothy] for endurance, that he may bear everything with fortitude and be ever in exercise (ἀσκήσει)."

In his exegesis of Phil. III, 14: "I press on toward the goal unto the prize of the high calling of God in Christ Jesus," St. Chrysostom brings out some interesting points which runners observe in their training. 62, 271, 45: "See how great a distance this is that must be run over (διαδραμεῖν)! . . . Do you see the runners, how they live by rule (νόμῳ), how they touch nothing that relaxes their strength, how they exercise themselves (ἀγωνίζονται) every day in the *palaestra* under a master (παιδοτρίβῃ) and by rule? Imitate them, or

---

[1]This alludes to the bruising of the face, or the parts under the eye in boxing.
[2]"Disqualified for the contest"—Goodspeed.

rather exhibit even greater eagerness, for the prizes are not equal. Many are those who would hinder you; live by rule. Many are the things which relax your strength; make your feet [*i. e.*, the feet of your strength] agile, for it is possible so to do; it comes not naturally, but by our will. Let us bring it to lightness, lest the weight of other things hinders our swiftness of foot. Teach your feet to be sure, for there are many slippery places; and if you fall, straightway you lose much. But yet if you fall, rise again. Even thus may you obtain the victory. Run upon firm ground; up with your head, up with your eyes; these commands the trainers (παιδοτρίβαι) give to those who run. Thus your strength is supported; but if you stoop, you fall, you are relaxed. Look upward, where the prize (βραβεῖον) is; the sight of the prize increases the determination of our will. The hope of taking it suffers us not to perceive the toils; it makes the distance appear short.''

As the runner looks to his instructor, so should the Christian keep his eyes fixed on Christ, as the admonition is in Heb. XII, 2. 63, 193, 36: "In the next place he mentions as the sum and substance of his exhortation, which he puts both first and last, even Christ . . . . 'Looking' (he says), that is, that we may learn to run. For as in the games (ἀγωνισμάτων), we impress the act upon our mind by looking to the masters (διδασκάλους), receiving certain rules through our sight, so here also, if we wish to run and to learn to run well, let us look to Christ, even to Jesus 'the author and perfecter of our faith.'''

God's method of training His athletes is similar in several respects to that of the trainers. For the comfort of those who have fallen (52, 522, 41) St. Chrysostom shows how God is preparing them, so that they will easily break the holds of their opponents. "The present life is a *palaestra*, a training and a contest (γυμνάσιον καὶ ἀγών) for virtue. . . . The trainers (παιδοτρίβαι) exercise the athletes in the *palaestra* with many toils, making a rather strenuous attack on those who are wrestling, in order that, having perfected everything in the training by practising on the bodies of their teachers, the athletes may be ready (εὐτρεπεῖς) for the contests and be prepared for the grips (λαβάς) of their opponents and easily break these (διαλύσωσιν). Thus does God in the present life.''

An excellent example of Christ's hunger being a hold which was given the devil in Christ's wrestling against him is presented (57, 210, 14) in the interpretation of St. Matt. IV, 2. "Having then fasted forty days and as many nights, He 'afterward hungered' affording the devil a point to lay hold of (λαβήν) and approach, that by actual conflict (συμπλακείς) He might show how to prevail and be victorious. Just so do wrestlers (ἀθληταί). When teaching their pupils (μαθητάς) how to prevail and overcome, they voluntarily in the lists (παλαίστραις) engage with (συμπλέκονται) others to afford these, in the persons (σώμασι) of their antagonists (ἀντιπάλων), the means of seeing and learning the mode of conquest. This same thing also took place. For it being His will to draw the devil on so far, He both made His hunger known to him and awaited his approach; and, as He waited for him, so Christ dashed him to earth, once, twice, thrice, with such ease as became Him."

Trainers also teach their pupils how to stand firmly. This point is illustrated in the comment on Eph. VI, 14: "Stand therefore, having girded your loins with truth . . . ." 62, 163, 42: "It is a great point to know how to stand. For in the case of wrestlers and boxers (πυκτευόντων καὶ παλαιόντων), the trainer (παιδοτρίβης) recommends this before everything else, namely, to stand firm (τὸ ἑστάναι)."

The serious-minded athlete makes no public display of his doings, but looks only to his trainer. This point is driven home to those who are vainglorious about almsgiving. 58, 665, 41: "In every matter, indeed, vainglory is a bad thing, yet most of all in beneficence, for it is the utmost cruelty, making a show of the calamities of others and all but upbraiding those in poverty. . . . We shall escape this danger, if we see after whose good report we are to seek. For tell me, who has the skill of almsgiving? Plainly, it is God, who has made known the thing, who best of all knows it and practises it without limit. What then? If you are learning to be a wrestler (παλαιστής), to whom do you look or to whom do you display your doings in the wrestling-school (παλαίστρᾳ), to the seller of herbs and of fish or to the trainer (παιδοτρίβῃ)? . . . . What then, if, while he [the trainer] admires you, others deride you, will you not with him deride them? What, if you are learning to box (πυκτεύειν), will you not look in like manner to him who knows how to teach this? How then is it other than absurd in other arts to look to the teacher only, but here to do the contrary, although the loss is not equal? For there, if you wrestle according to the opinion of the multitude, but not that of the teacher, the loss is in the wrestling; but here it is in eternal life. You are become like God in giving alms; be then like Him in not making a display."

Our training is gradual and preliminary exercise should make it possible to bear not only the severity of words, but also affliction itself. There is an interesting comment on II Thess. I, 7, 8: "... in flaming fire, rendering vengeance to them that know not God ...." 62, 477, 56: "If no one endures a discourse concerning hell, it is evident that, if persecution arises, no one would ever stand firm against fire or sword. Let us exercise (γυμνάσωμεν) our ears not to be over soft and tender, for from this we shall come to endure even the things themselves."

God did not appear to St. Paul until he fell into danger. In Acts XXIII, 6–11 there is so great a dissension between the Pharisees and Saducees concerning the teachings of St. Paul that his life was endangered. 60, 341, 52: "God did not appear to Paul before he fell into danger, because He appears more desired in afflictions and also in dangers He exercises and trains (ἐγγυμνάζει) us."

The necessity of practising beforehand in the case of virtue as in the various athletic arts is emphasized in 60, 220, 32. "If we practised ourselves (ἐγυμναζόμεθα) beforehand in the case of all our passions, we should not make a ridiculous figure (καταγέλαστοι) in the contests (ἀγῶσιν) themselves. But now we have our implements and our exercises (γυμνάσια) and our trainings for other things, for arts and feats of the *palaestra* (παλαισμάτων), but for virtue nothing of the sort. And yet we, though in all respects unpractised, wish for the first prizes!"

The art of the charioteer is used quite effectively (60, 220, 4) as an example for the necessity of practising beforehand. This is prefaced by a metaphor on wrestling. "God has so arranged that all the passions do not set upon us at one and the same time of life. They are divided and discribed, so that our wrestling with them will not be made more difficult. What wretched inertness it shows, not to be able to conquer our passions even when taken one by one? ... Whence is it that throughout life we continually fail in every encounter? We have never practised this art of the charioteer. Never in a time of leisure, when there is no contest (ἀγῶνος), have we talked over with ourselves what shall be useful for us. We are never seen in our place on the chariot, until the time for the contest (ἀγών) is actually come. Hence the ridiculous figure we make there. Have I not often said, 'Let us practise ourselves (γυμναζώμεθα) upon those of our own family before the time of trial'? .... Look at the chariot-drivers (ἡνιόχους); do you not see how exceedingly careful and strict they are with themselves in their training-practice (γυμνασία), their labors, their diet, and all the rest, that they may not be thrown from their chariots and dragged along [by the reins]? See what a thing art is!"

Before being admitted into the Church candidates received instruction for a period of thirty days. This length of time is compared with a wrestling-school where they practise the exercises beforehand and so learn how to get the better of the evil demon. 49, 228, 20: "May you always remain in preservation of the beauty and the brightness, which you are now about to receive, unsullied. In order, then, that you may ever remain thus, come, let us discourse to you a little about your manner of life. For in the wrestling-schools (παλαίστρᾳ) falls (πτώματα) of the athletes are devoid of danger. For the wrestling is with friends, and they practise all their exercises on the persons of their teachers. But when the time of the contest (ἀγώνων) has come, when the lists (στάδιον) are open, when the spectators are seated above, when the president (ἀγωνοθέτης) has arrived, it necessarily follows that the combatants, if they become careless (ῥᾳθυμήσαντας), fall and retire in great disgrace; or, if they are in earnest (σπουδάσαντας), win the crowns and the prizes (τῶν στεφάνων καὶ τῶν βραβείων ἐπιτυχεῖν). So then, in your case, these thirty days are like some wrestling-school both for exercise and practice: let us learn from there already to get the better of that evil demon. For it is to contend with him that we must strip ourselves, with him after baptism must we box (πυκτεύειν) and fight. Let us learn from there already his grip (λαβάς), on what side he is aggressive, on what side he can easily threaten us, in order that when the contest (ἀγώνων) comes, we may not feel strange or become confused, as seeing new forms of wrestling (καινὰ τὰ παλαίσματα), but that, having already practised them among ourselves and having learned all his methods, we may with courage engage in these forms of wrestling against him."

He who desires to have his soul trained as well as his body must ever keep in practice. I Tim. IV, 8: "for bodily exercise is profitable for a little . . . ." 62, 560, 13: "What we need is the exercise (γυμνασίας) of the soul. For the exercise of the body may benefit the body a little while, but the exercise (ἄσκησις)[1] of godliness yields fruit and advantage both here and hereafter. He who exercises himself (γυμναζόμενος), even when it is not the season of contest (ἀγώνων), acts always as if contending (ἀγωνιζόμενος), practises abstinence, endures all toils (ἐναγώνιος), endures much labor."

Unless real preparation has been made for the conflicts of life, baptism is not always so productive as it was designed to be. 60, 25,

---

[1] The proper word for spiritual exercise. St. Paul uses the other (γυμνασία), because bodily exercise for bodily purposes was familiar to all Greeks.

13: "When a man is sick, he is baptised, and, if he recovers from his illness, he is as vexed (ἐπηρεασθείς, 'cheated of his prize'), as if some great harm has been done him. For since he has not been prepared for a virtuous life, he has no heart for the conflicts (ἀγῶνας) which will follow and he shrinks at the thought of them. Christ gave us baptism, not that we should receive it and depart, but that we should show the fruits of it in our after-life."

Similarly, results are expected from church-going. 60, 217, 61: "Church-going is in vain, unless some fruit is reaped from it. Behold the wrestler (ἀθλητής), who by frequenting the gymnastic ground (παλαίστραν) becomes more skilful in wrestling (περὶ τὴν πάλην)!"

St. Paul, our training-master, through his Epistles gives instructions about overcoming our antagonists and shows how nothing can be of profit, if it is not accompanied by practice. 51, 179, 57: "Let us then adorn our inward man and let us be mindful of the things which are said here [in church], when we go out: for there especially is it a proper time to remember them; and just as an athlete displays in the lists (ἀγώνων) the things which he has learned in the training-school (ἐπὶ τῆς παλαίστρας), even so ought we to display in our transactions in the world without the things which we have heard here. Bear in mind then the things said here, that, when you have gone out and the devil lays hold of you by means of either anger or vainglory or any other passion, you may call to remembrance the teaching which you have received here and may be able easily to shake off the grasp of the evil one. Do you not see the wrestling-masters (παιδοτρίβας) in the practising-grounds (σκάμμασι), who after countless contests (ἄθλους) have obtained exemption from wrestling on account of their age, sitting outside the lines (σκαμμά-των) by the side of the dust and shouting to those who are wrestling inside, telling one to grasp a hand or to drag a leg or to seize upon the back, and by many other directions of that kind saying, 'If you do so and so, you will easily throw your antagonist (ἐκτενεῖς τὸν ἀνταγωνιστήν),' and so being of the greatest service to their pupils? Even so look to your training-master, the blessed Paul, who after countless victories now sits outside the boundary (σκάμματος)—I mean of this present life—and cries aloud to us who are wrestling, shouting out by means of his Epistles, when he sees us overcome by wrath and resentment of injuries and choked by passion: 'If thine enemy hunger, feed him [Rom. XII, 20].' And exactly as the training-master says that, if you do so and so, you will overcome your antagonist, so he also adds, 'For in so doing thou shalt heap coals of fire upon his head [ib.].'"

If the athlete in his training has not become used to a trainer, he will not be able to make a good showing against his antagonist; so there is need of proper training for those who are to take part in the Christian contests. 57, 395, 15: "If now it should happen (as I pray that it may not) that there should be a war against churches and a persecution, imagine how great the ridicule and how sore the reproaches. And very naturally; for when no one exercises himself (γυμνάζηται) in the wrestling-school (παλαίστρᾳ), how will he be distinguished (λαμπρός) in the contests (ἀγῶσιν)? What champion (ἀθλητής), not being used to the trainer (παιδοτρίβην), will be able, when summoned by the Olympic contests, to show forth anything great and noble against his antagonist (ἀνταγωνιστήν)? Ought we not every day to wrestle and fight and run? Do you not see those who are called *pentathli* (πεντάθλους), when they have no antagonists, how they fill a sack (θύλακον) with much sand and hanging it up try their full strength (γυμνάζουσιν) thereupon? And they that are still younger practise upon the persons of their companions. These do you also emulate and practise the wrestlings of self-denial. For indeed there are many that provoke to anger and incite to lust and kindle a great flame. Stand therefore against your passions, bear nobly the mental pangs, that you may endure also those of the body. For so the blessed Job, if he had not exercised himself (ἦν γυμνασάμενος) well before his conflicts (ἀγώνων), would not have shown so brightly in the same. . . . And if you would see his ways of exercise (γυμνάσια) also, hear him saying how he used to despise wealth: 'If I have rejoiced,' says he, 'because my wealth was great . . . if I have made gold my hope, if I have put my trust in precious stone [Job XXXI, 25, 24, LXX].' Therefore was he not confounded at their being taken away, since he desired them not when present. And if you would also hear of his strivings (ἀγῶνας) after continence (σωφροσύνης), hearken to him when he says, 'I made a covenant with mine eyes, that I should not look upon a virgin [Job XXXI, 1].' . . . Wherefore I am led even to marvel, whence it came into the devil's thought to stir up the contest (ἀγῶνας), knowing as he did of his previous training (γυμνάσια)."

It is God's method to allow His athletes to undergo a period of training before winning the rewards. Acts VII, 6, 7: "And God spake on this wise, that his [Abraham's] seed should sojourn in a strange land, and that they should bring them into bondage, and treat them ill, four hundred years. And the nation to which they shall be in bondage will I judge, said God: and after that shall they come forth, and serve me in this place." 50, 127, 20: "He who gave the land permits first the evils. So also now, though He has promised a kingdom, yet He suffers us to be exercised (ἐγγυμνάζεσθαι) in temptations."

All God's athletes must be trained, and even those who are noble and approved, such as Abraham, are not exempt. Heb. XI, 17: "By faith Abraham, being tried, offered up Isaac . . . ." 63, 173, 22: "Although God knew that Abraham was noble and approved (δόκιμος), He tempted him that He might make his fortitude manifest to all. . . . If then temptations make men so approved (δοκίμους) that, even where there is no occasion, God exercises (γυμνάζειν) His own athletes, much more ought we to bear all things nobly."

The test of real preparation is that virtue, like an athlete, must be prepared for everything. This is well exemplified in the case of the Apostles. 62, 275, 6: "The Apostles worked in every state, 'by glory and dishonor, by evil report and good report [II Cor. VI, 8].' This is an athlete, to be prepared (ἐπιτήδειον) for everything: for such is also the nature of virtue."

Job as a result of his training obtained greater boldness in speech. 64, 536, 21: "God not only deprived him of his goods, but He made him a far richer man in virtue. For having been trained in a greater contest (ἀγωνισάμενος ἀγῶνα), he was afterward rendered more bold in speech (πλείονος παρρησίας)."

Simple living and strenuous exercise have as good results for the Christian as for the athlete. When St. Paul came to Corinth, he lived with Aquila, a tentmaker, with whom he practised his craft. 60, 277, 58: "Smile not, beloved, to hear of his occupation. For it was good for him, even as to the athlete the *palaestra* is more useful than delicate carpets."

After the athlete is fully prepared, he is ready to be anointed and to enter the contest. Such was the case of our Lord's disciples. 59, 409, 13: "For they who now trembled and feared, after they had received the Spirit, sprang into the midst of dangers and stripped themselves for the contest against steel and fire and wild beasts and seas and every kind of punishment."

The Holy Spirit is the Anointer of the disciples, according to the comment on St. John XIV, 16: "And I will pray the Father, and he shall give you another Comforter, that he may be with you for ever." 59, 404, 44: "When the disciples were being sent forth to dangers and were stripping themselves for the contest (ἀγῶνας), then need was that the Anointer (ἀλείφοντα) should come." St. Paul also is represented as anointing the spirits of the Corinthians once more for the combat in II Cor. I, 11: "ye also helping together on our behalf by your supplication . . . ." 61, 396, 44, and 398, 20: "Thus having shown the gain of affliction and then having made them energetic (ἐναγωνίους), he anoints (ἀλείφει) once more their spirits [for the combat] and animates them to virtue by witnessing great things of their prayers. . . . Let us then be diligent in coming together in supplication; and let us pray for one another, as they did for the Apostles. For so we both fulfill a commandment and are anointed (ἀλειφόμεθα) to love,—and when I speak of love, I speak of every good thing."

Christ's promises of good things to come were for the purpose of anointing His followers for the contest, as St. Chrysostom interprets Heb. III, 6: ". . . whose [Christ's] house are we, if we hold fast our boldness and the glorying of our hope firm unto the end." 63, 50, 48: "Christ told us of the good things beforehand, in order that by the promise He might refresh (ἀνακτήσηται) our souls, that by the engagement He might strengthen our zeal, that He might anoint us [for our contests] and stir up (διεγείρῃ) our mind."

Quite similar is God's way of preparing St. Paul for the contest. 57, 402, 53: "He anointed (ἀλείψας) His pupil [St. Paul], both by opening heaven to him and by setting before him that fearful judgment-seat and by pointing to the amphitheatre of angels and [by showing] how in the midst of them the crowns shall be proclaimed (ἀνακήρυξιν τῶν στεφάνων)."

Being forgiven one's trespasses enables one to put off the "old man" and to be anointed so that one can enter the lists. 62, 342, 13: "Man puts off the 'old man' as easily as his garments before going up [to the contest]. He is anointed as wrestlers (ἀθληταί) about to enter the lists (στάδιον). . . . He comes to wrestle and to be exercised (ἀθλήσων καὶ γυμνασθησόμενος); he is advanced to another creation. For when one confesses his belief in the life everlasting, one has confessed a second creation."

They who labor in teaching should be counted worthy of a particularly great honor. Commenting on I Cor. I, 17: "For Christ sent me not to baptize, but to preach the gospel . . . ," St. Chrysostom says (61, 26, 40): "Baptism is intrusted to the elders, but preaching to the wiser." He then quotes I Tim. V, 17: "Let the elders that rule well be counted worthy of double honor, especially those who labor in the word and in teaching." Continuing the comment we read, "For as to teach the wrestlers in the games is the part of a spirited and skillful trainer (γενναίου καὶ παιδοτρίβου σοφοῦ), but to place the crown on the conqueror's head may be that of one who cannot even wrestle (although it is the crown which adds splendor to the conqueror), so also in baptism. It is impossible to be saved without it, yet it is no great thing which the baptizer does, finding the will ready prepared.''

The idea that a teacher may not lose the dignity which is becoming to him is conveyed in the comment on Gal. VI, 6: ''. . . let him that is taught in the word communciate unto him that teacheth in all good things.'' 61, 676, 10: ''For inasmuch as the dignity of a teacher ofttimes elates him who possesses it, He, in order to repress his spirit, has imposed on him the necessity of requiring aid at the hands of his disciples. And to these in turn He has given means of cultivating kindly feelings, by training (γυμνάζων) them, through the kindness required of them to their teachers, in gentleness toward others also.''

That God as the Christian Trainer is always busy is inferred from II Cor. I, 3, 4: ''Blessed be the God . . . the Father of mercies and God of all comfort; who comforteth us in all our affliction, that we may be able to comfort them that are in any affliction . . . .'' 61, 386, 38: ''Hereby also he manifests the excellency of the Apostles, showing that, having been comforted and breathed (ἀναπνεύσας) awhile, he lies not softly down as we, but goes on his way to anoint (ἀλείφειν), to nerve, to rouse others.''

Several instances of Christ's training His disciples occur in St. Chrysostom's *Homiliae in S. Matthaeum.*

St. Matt. V, 14, 15: ''. . . A city set on a hill cannot be hid. Neither do men light a lamp, and put it under the bushel . . . .'' 57, 232, 31: ''Again by these words He trains them to strictness of life, teaching them to be earnest in their endeavors (ἐναγωνίους), as set before the eyes of all men and contending (ἀγωνιζομένους) in the midst of the amphitheatre of the world.''

St. Matt. VIII, 23, 24: ''And when he was entered into a boat, his disciples followed him. And behold, there arose a great tempest in the sea, insomuch that the boat was covered with the waves: but he was asleep.'' 57, 350, 42: ''And He took them with Him, not for nought or at hazard, but in order to make them spectators of the miracle that was to take place. For like a most excellent trainer (παιδοτρίβης ἄριστος), He was anoiṅting (ἤλειφεν) them with a view to both objects: as well to be undismayed in dangers, as to be modest (μετριάζειν) in honors. Thus, that they might not be high-minded, because, having sent away the rest, He retained them, He suffered them to be tossed with the tempest, at once correcting this and disciplining (γυμνάζων) them to bear trials nobly. For great indeed were the former miracles too, but this contained also in it a kind of discipline (γυμνασίαν), and that no inconsiderable one, and was a sign akin to that of old.[1] For this cause He took only the disciples with Him. For as, when there was a display of miracles, He suffered the people also to be present, so when trials and terrors were rising against Him, then He took with Him none but the champions (ἀθλητάς) of the whole world, whom He was to discipline (γυμνάζειν)."

St. Matt. IX, 37, 38: ". . . The harvest indeed is plenteous, but the laborers are few. Pray ye therefore the Lord of the harvest, that he send forth laborers into his harvest." 57, 379, 26: "He sent out His disciples, that He might teach them, after practising in Palestine, as in a sort of training-school (παλαίστρᾳ), to strip themselves for their conflicts (ἀγῶνας) with the world. For this purpose then He made the exercises (γυμνάσια) even more serious than the actual conflicts (ἀγώνων), so far as pertained to their own virtue, that they might more easily engage (ἄψωνται) in the struggles (ἀγώνων) that were to ensue."

St. Matt. X, 12, 13: "And as ye enter into the house, salute it. And if the house be worthy, let your peace come upon it: but if it be not worthy, let your peace return to you." 57, 383, 33: "Do you see how far He does not hesitate to carry His injunctions? And very fitly; for as champions (ἀθλητάς) of godliness and preachers to the whole world was He training them."

St. Matt. X, 23: "But when they persecute you in this city, flee into the next: for verily I say unto you, Ye shall not have gone through the cities of Israel, till the Son of man be come." 57, 397, 35: "Having spoken of those fearful and horrible things, enough to melt very adamant, which after His cross and resurrection and assumption were to befall them, He directs again His discourse to what was of more tranquil character, allowing those whom He is training (ἀθλη-ταῖς) to recover breath (ἀναπνεῦσαι) and affording them full assurance."

St. Matt. X, 32: "Every one therefore who shall confess me before men, him will I also confess before my Father who is in heaven." 57, 402, 4: "But why is He not satisfied with the faith in the mind, but requires also the confession with the mouth?—to anoint (ἀλείφων) us to boldness in speech and a more abundant love and determination

---

[1] *I. e.*, the miracle at the Red Sea.

and to raise us on high. From the things here form your conjecture also about things to come. Why, if in the season of the conflicts (ἀγώνων) they that confess are so glorious, imagine what they will be in the season of the crowns. If the enemies here applaud, how shall that tenderest of all fathers fail to admire and proclaim you (θαυμάσεταί σε καὶ ἀνακηρύξει)?"

St. Matt. XVII, 1–3: "... Jesus taketh with him Peter, and James, and John his brother, and bringeth them up into a high mountain apart: and he was transfigured before them .... And behold, there appeared unto them Moses and Elijah talking with him." 58, 552, 58: "For not into Egypt did they [the disciples] enter, but into the whole world, worse disposed than the Egyptians; nor were they to speak with Pharaoh, but to fight hand to hand (πυκτεύσοντες) with the devil, the very prince of wickedness. Yea, and their appointed struggle (ἀγών) was both to bind him and to spoil all his goods; and this they did cleaving not the sea, but an abyss of ungodliness, through the rod of Jesse,—an abyss having waves far more grievous. ... To anoint (ἀλείφων) them therefore for all this He brought forward those who shone forth under the old law."

St. Matt. XIX, 27: "Then answered Peter, and said unto him, Lo, we have left all, and followed thee; what then shall we have?" 58, 611, 38: "When He had then raised the spirit of all and had persuaded them to feel confidence both with respect to themselves and to all the world, He added, 'But many shall be last that are first; and first that are last [St. Matt. XIX, 30].' ... Then He adds also a parable [of the laborers, St. Matt. XX, 1–16], as anointing (ἀλείφων) those who had fallen short (ὑστερηκότας) to a great forwardness (προθυμίαν)."

St. Matt. XX, 17–19: "And as Jesus was going up to Jerusalem, he took the twelve disciples apart, and on the way he said unto them, Behold, we go up to Jerusalem; and the Son of man shall be delivered unto the chief priests and scribes; and they shall condemn him to death, and shall deliver him unto the Gentiles to mock, and to scourge, and to crucify: and the third day he shall be raised up." 58, 617, 27: "He was continually putting them in remembrance, exercising (ἐγγυμνάζων) their mind by the frequency with which He reminded them and diminishing their pain ... and that it might not confound them by coming upon them without preparation. So for this cause, while in the beginning He spoke of His death only, when they were practised and trained (ἐνεγυμνάσαντο) to hear of it, He added the other circumstances also."

St. Matt. XXI, 19, 20: "And seeing a fig tree by the way side, he came to it, and found nothing thereon, but leaves only; and he saith unto it, Let there be no fruit from thee henceforward for ever. And immediately the fig tree withered away. And when the disciples saw it, they marvelled, saying, How did the fig tree immediately wither away?" 58, 634, 22: "And that you might learn that for their sakes this was done, that He might anoint (ἀλείψῃ) them to feel confidence, hear what He said afterward: 'You also shall do greater things, if you are willing to believe and to be confident in prayer [St. Matt. XXI, 21, 22, paraphrased].'"

PART II. THE CONTEST

The contest proper, as one may naturally suppose, consists of the usual three primary feats of skill and strength: running, wrestling and boxing. To these has been added the chariot-race, which is one of the most exciting and thrilling parts of the games and is used quite effectively by St. Chrysostom for emphasizing certain points which the Christian Athlete may apply to make his contest more successful. There are a certain number of references where the nature of the contest seems to be indefinite and which do not admit of specific application in any one of the four major contests; so they are put in a section by themselves under the title of "The Contest in General."[1] The regulations of the games and the functions of the presiding official will be treated in the first chapter, as the succeeding chapters will thus be better elucidated. The Contest, then, will be divided into six chapters, as follows: 1. Regulations of the Games and Functions of the Presiding Official, 2. Running, 3. Wrestling, 4. Boxing, 5. Chariot-Racing, 6. The Contest in General.

---

[1]In the Biblical Homilies St. Chrysostom makes no reference to javelin-throwing, discus-throwing and jumping,—the other categories of the Olympic games.

1. REGULATIONS OF THE GAMES AND FUNCTIONS OF THE PRESIDING OFFICIAL

In some respects the regulations of the Christian Contest are in accordance with those of the Olympic Games. These will be noted presently. However, there are points where the regulations of Christ's stadium are different, as is elaborated in the exegesis of Rom. XII, 21: "Be not overcome of evil, but overcome evil with good." 60, 613, 26: "Christ has given us laws upon all these points for our good and has shown us what makes us have a good name, what brings us to disgrace.... If then He both cares and knows, why do you quarrel with Him and wish to go another road? For conquering by doing ill is one of the devil's laws. Hence in the Olympic games which were celebrated to him[1] it is so ordered that all the competitors conquer. But in Christ's stadium this is not the rule about the prize, for, on the contrary, the law is for the person smitten, and not for the person smiting, to be crowned. For such is the character of His stadium; it has all its regulations the other way, so that it is not in the victory only, but also in the way of the victory, that the marvel is the greater. For when things, which on the one side are signs of defeat, on the other side show victory: this is the power of God, this the stadium of heaven, this the theatre of angels."

The athlete must be tried in order to be approved in the contests. Rom. V, 3: "... tribulation worketh steadfastness" is quoted in this connection. 60, 255, 57: "Nothing can be more worthless than a man who passes all his time in idleness and luxury. For the man untried (ἀπείραστος), as the saying is, is also unapproved (ἀδόκιμος); unapproved not only in the contests (ἀγῶσι), but also in everything else."

Those about to partake of the Eucharist should not come to the spiritual fountain carelessly and in a chance way, but should be qualified like the athlete who is to participate in the games. 63, 133, 9: "Tell me then, I beseech you, in the Olympic games does not the herald stand, calling out with loud and uplifted voice, saying, 'Does any one accuse this man? Is he a slave? Is he a thief? Is he one of wicked manners?' And yet those contests (ἀγωνίσματα) for prizes are not of the soul, nor yet of good morals, but of strength and the body. If then, where there is exercise (ἄσκησις) of bodies,

---

[1]The Fathers generally believed that the devils were connected with idolatry: v. especially St. Augustine, *De Civitate Dei*, I, 32.

much examination is made about character, how much rather here, where the soul is alone the combatant (ἀθλεῖ)? Our herald [the priest] then even now stands, not holding each person by the head and drawing him forward, but holding all together by the head within; he does not set against them other accusers, but themselves against themselves. For he says not, 'Does any one accuse this man?' But what? 'If any man accuses himself.' For when he says, 'The holy things for the holy,' he means this: 'If any one is not holy, let him not draw near.'"

No athlete is disqualified because of looks; so bodily accidents do not affect one who is enrolled in the New Covenant. Such is the comment on Gal. V, 6: "For in Christ Jesus neither circumcision availeth anything, nor uncircumcision; but faith working through love." 61, 666, 22: "It is faith that makes the difference. As in the selection of athletes (ἀθλητάς), whether hook-nosed (γρυπούς) or flat-nosed (σιμούς), black or white, is of no importance in their trial (δοκιμασίαν); it is only necessary to seek that they should be strong and skillful (ἰσχυροὶ καὶ ἐπιστήμονες). So all these bodily accidents (σωματικά) do not injure one who will be enrolled under the New Covenant, nor does their presence assist him."

The athlete must be temperate not only while in training, but also at the time of the contest itself. This remark is quite naturally made on I Cor. IX, 25: "And every man that striveth in the games (ἀγωνι-ζόμενος) exerciseth self-control (ἐγκρατεύεται) in all things. . . ." 61, 189, 21: "What is 'all things'? He does not abstain from one and err in another, but he masters entirely gluttony (γαστρι-μαργίας) and lasciviousness (λαγνείας) and drunkenness and all his passions. 'For this,' says he, 'takes place even in the heathen games (τῶν ἔξωθεν ἀγώνων). For neither is excess of wine (μεθύειν) permitted to those who contend at the time of the contest nor wantonness (πορνεύειν), lest they should weaken their vigor (τὴν δύναμιν ἐκλύσωσιν), nor yet so much as to be busied about anything else, but separating themselves altogether from all things they apply themselves to their exercise (γυμνασίοις) only.' Now if there these things are so where the crown falls to one, much more here, where the incitement in emulation is more abundant. For here one is not crowned alone; and the rewards (ἔπαθλα) also far surpass the labors."

Also in 62, 294, 42 the athlete must live according to rule. "Do you see how tribulation is everywhere lauded, everywhere assumed as needful for us? For if in the contests of the world no one without this receives the crown, unless he fortifies himself by toil, by abstinence from delicacies, by living according to rule (νόμῳ διαίτης), by watchings and by innumerable other things, much more so here."

The use of vigilance in the games is most vividly portrayed in 63, 116, 22. "Many of you have often beheld the Olympic games; and have not only beheld but also been zealous partisans and admirers (σπουδασταί καὶ θαυμασταί) of the combatants (ἀγωνιζομένων), one of this combatant, one of that. You know then that, both during the days of the contests (ἀγώνων) and during the nights, all night long the herald thinks of nothing else, has no other anxiety than that the combatant should not disgrace himself when he goes forth. . . . . If therefore he, who is about to strive (ἀγωνίζεσθαι) before men, uses such forethought, much more will it befit us continually to be thoughtful and careful, since our whole life is a contest (ἀγών). Let every night then be a vigil, and let us be careful that, when we go out in the day, we do not make ourselves ridiculous. But now the Judge of the contest (ἀγωνοθέτης) is seated on the right hand of the Father; and He is the Judge not only of actions but also of words. . . . . Wherefore, I exhort you, let us lay aside all other things and look to one only, how we may obtain the prize (βραβεῖον) and how we may be wreathed with the crown."

Although the athletes have the best of attention when engaged in the contest, yet they do not enjoy entire ease. This is the comment on Heb. XI, 13: "These all died in faith, not having received the promises. . ." 63, 162, 1: "Christ said, 'Seek ye the kingdom of God, and all these things shall be added unto you [St. Matt. VI, 33].' Do you see that these things are given by Him in the way of addition, that we may not faint? For as the athletes have the benefit of careful attention (θεραπείας), even when engaged in the combat (ἀγωνίζωνται), but do not enjoy entire ease (ἀνέσεως), since they must live under rules (νόμοις), yet afterward they enjoy it entire; so God also does not grant us here to partake of entire ease."

The method of choosing opponents in the games is found in 64, 881, 21. "In the beginning there was an allotment of ministry and apostleship. The origin seems to have been the placing of a name on him who was elected first. Or, as in the Olympic games, one was chosen by lot to have this antagonist (ἀνταγωνιστήν), another that one. . . . As each one has so been given his lot by God, so let him walk."

Attention is now directed to the presiding official. Those who presided at the games were men of distinction and wealth, since they usually furnished the spectacles at their own expense.[1] When Antioch was punished in 387 for her sedition, these men were numbered among the chief ones of the city who suffered most severely. 49, 139, 9: "At last having loaded the culprits with chains and bound them with iron, they [the judges] sent them away to the prison through the midst of the forum. Men who had kept their studs of horses (ἱπποτρόφους), who had been presidents of the games (ἀγωνοθέτας), who could reckon ten thousand different offices of distinction (μυρίας λειτουργίας) which they had held, had their goods confiscated, and seals might be seen placed upon all their doors."

The prominence of these presidents may also be inferred from St. Chrysostom's arraignment of the people for knowing all about the things of the world, but nothing about the city of God. 57, 23, 1: "You know exactly the affairs of the world, as well new as old, and much too as are quite ancient; you can number the princes under whom you have served in time past, and the ruler of the games (ἀγωνοθέτην), and those who gained the prize (ἀθλοφόρους), and the leaders of armies,—matters that are of no concern to you; but who has become ruler in the city [of God], . . . you have not even imagined as in a dream."

A splendid example of acting as umpire or as judge[2] in the games occurs in the comment on Col. III, 15: "And let the peace of Christ rule (βραβευέτω) in your hearts . . . ." 62, 354, 48: "If two thoughts are fighting together, set not anger, set not spitefulness (ἐπήρειαν) to hold the prize (βραβεῖον), but peace; for instance, suppose one to have been insulted unjustly: of the insult are born two thoughts, the one bidding him to avenge, the other to endure; and these wrestle with each other: if the peace of God stands forward as umpire, it bestows the prize on that which bids endure and puts the other to shame. How?—by persuading him that God is peace, that He has

---

[1]Such were the Asiarchs mentioned in Acts XIX, 31.

[2]In the Olympic games the judges were appointed by popular election from among the Eleans themselves. Their number rose in the course of time from one to two, nine, ten, and twelve; but after 348 B. C. it was always ten. Distinguished by purple robes, wreaths of bay-leaves and a seat of honor opposite the stadium, they kept guard over the strict observance of all the minute regulations for the contests and in general maintained order. In these duties they were supported by a number of attendants provided with staves. Transgressions of the laws of the games and unfairness on the part of competitors were punished by forfeiture of the prize or by fines of money, which became a part of the revenue of the temple.

made peace with us. Not without reason he shows the great struggle (ἀγῶνα) there is in the matter. . . . He has represented an arena (στάδιον) within, in the thoughts, and a contest and a wrestling and an umpire (ἀγῶνα καὶ ἄθλησιν καὶ βραβευτήν). Then again, exhortation, 'to the which ye were called,' he says, that is, 'for the which ye were called.' He has reminded them of how many good things peace is the cause; on account of this He called you, for this He called you, so as to receive a worthy prize (ἀξιόπιστον τὸ βραβεῖον). . . . But why said he not, 'Let the peace of God be victorious (νικάτω),' but 'be umpire (βραβευέτω)'? He has made it [peace] the more honorable. He would not have the evil thought come to wrestle (προσπαλαίειν) with it, but stand below. And the very word *prize* cheered the hearer. For if it [peace] has given the prize to the good thought, however impudently the other behaves, the contest is thereafter of no use. And besides, the other [the evil thought] being aware that, perform what feats it might, it should not receive the prize, however it might puff and attempt still more vehement onsets, it would desist as laboring without profit."

Even though one has lawfully earned the prize, yet one may be robbed of it by means of threatening abuse. This is found in the interpretation of Col. II, 18: "Let no man rob you of your prize (καταβραβευέτω) by a voluntary humility and worshipping of the angels . . . ." 62, 343, 49: "Let no one adjudge away from you (καταβραβευέτω) the Body of Christ, that is, thwart you of it (ἐπηρεαζέτω). The word καταβραβευθῆναι is employed when the victory is with one party and the prize (βραβεῖον) with another: when, though a victor, you are thwarted. You stand above the devil and sin; why do you again subject yourself to sin?"

Christ is represented as the presiding official in 58, 792, 37, where poverty is enjoined. "Learn this from the Master of the conflicts (ἀγωνοθέτου) Himself, what He said to the rich man seeking eternal life: 'Sell that which thou hast, and give to the poor, and come follow me, and thou shalt have treasure in heaven [St. Matt. XIX, 21].'"

God is the judge of Job when the latter says (Job XVI, 20), "My friends scoff at me: But mine eye poureth out tears unto God." 64, 620, 2: "The great Judge (ὁ μέγας ἀγωνοθέτης) watched your contests (παλαίσματα) and heard your supplication and viewed your precious tears, and therefore the cause of the contests (ἀγώνων) He made certain and manifest to all."

The master of the games must be impartial and give the prizes only to those who obtained them by labor. This is learned from the exposition of Christ's reply to the two sons of Zebedee in St. Matt. XX, 23: "...My cup indeed ye shall drink [and be baptized with the baptism that I am baptized with]: but to sit on my right hand, and on my left hand, is not mine to give: but it is for them for whom it hath been prepared of my Father." 58, 621, 1:"And in order that what I say may be more plain, let us work (γυμνάσωμεν) it on an illustration and let us suppose that there would be some master of the games (ἀγωνοθέτην), then that many excellent combatants (ἀθλητὰς ἀρίστους) would go down to the contest (ἀγῶνα), and that some two of the combatants who were most nearly connected with the master of the games would go to him and say, 'Cause us to be crowned and proclaimed (ἀνακηρυχθῆναι),' confiding in their good-will and friendship with him, and that he would say to them, 'This is not mine to give, but it shall be given to them for whom it is prepared, by their labors and their toils,' should we indeed condemn him as powerless? By no means; but we should approve him for his justice and for having no respect of persons. We should not say that he did not give the crown from want of vigor, but from not wishing to corrupt the law of the games (ἀγώνων) or to disturb the order of justice."

2. RUNNING[1]

The foot-race was regarded as the lightest of the contests, and for this reason must be run with patience, as in Heb. XII, 1, 2: ". . . let us run with patience the race that is set before us, looking unto Jesus the author and perfecter of our faith." 63, 193, 31: "He did not say, 'Let us contend as boxers (πυκτεύωμεν)' or 'Let us wrestle (παλαίω-μεν)': but, what was lightest of all, the contest of the foot-race (δρόμου). Nor yet did he say, 'Let us add to the length of the course,' but 'Let us continue patiently in this, let us not faint.'"

The race must be run, and so we need grace from above for it, Rom. IX, 16: ". . . it is not of him that willeth, nor of him that runneth, but of God that hath mercy." 60, 561, 24: "Paul shows that all is not one's own, for it requires grace from above. For it is binding on us to will and also to run: but to confide not in our own labors, but in the love of God toward man."

Women as well as men run the race,[2]—in fact, they put men to shame by being crowned as they carry on the races that Apostles and Evangelists ran. This is declared in the comment on Rom. XVI, 6: "Salute Mary, who bestowed much labor on you." 60, 668, 54: "A woman again is crowned and proclaimed victorious (ἀνακηρύττεται)! . . . Such women put us men to shame that we are left so far behind by them (ἀπολιμπανόμεθα). But if we come to know whence it comes that they are so adorned, we too shall speedily overtake them (καταληψόμεθα). . . . Whence then is their adornment? It is from their toils (ἱδρώτων) in behalf of the truth, . . . so carrying on (ἀναδεξάμεναι) races (δρόμους) that Apostles and Evangelists ran."

Several kinds of courses are mentioned. The priesthood is compared with a course to which St. Basil was dragged by craft. St.

---

[1]In the first Olympiad the contest consisted of a simple match in the stadium (race-course), which had a length of a trifle more than 210 yards. The runners ran in heats of four, after which the winners in each heat competed together, the first in the final heat being proclaimed victor. About 724 B. C. the double course (δίαυλος) was introduced, in which the runners had to make a circuit of the goal and return to the starting-point. About 720 came the δόλιχος, or long race, where the distance of the stadium had to be covered either six, seven, eight, twelve, twenty, or twenty-nine times. In 520 began the practice of the race in armor, with helmet, greaves and shield, though later the shield alone was carried. Competitors ran barefooted and bareheaded. The start of the running-track was marked by two parallel grooves a few inches apart. The signal to start was given by the herald calling "Go" (ἄπιτε), or, perhaps (as in the chariot-race), by a blast of the trumpet.

[2]Because of the great concern that a mother has for her children, she is said to have a long double course (μακροὺς διαύλους) in 63, 488, 53.

Chrysostom tells how this happened in 48, 638, 15. "Basil had at one time said, 'I do not know how otherwise to love than by giving up my life, when it is necessary to save any of my friends who are in danger,' thus repeating in different words indeed, but with the same meaning,what Christ said to His disciples, when He laid down the definition of perfect love: 'Greater love,' He said, 'hath no man than this, that a man lay down his life for his friends [St. John XV, 13].' If then it is impossible to find greater love than this, you have attained its limit and by both your deeds and words have crowned the summit. This is why I betrayed you; this is why I contrived that plot. Do I now convince you that it was not from any malicious intent or from any desire to thrust you into danger, but from a persuasion of your future usefulness that I dragged you into this course (στάδιον)?"

St. Paul's journey to Jerusalem is called a course. St. Paul did not know the things that would befall him on his way to Jerusalem, but nothing moved him from the resolve to finish his course with joy. 60, 311, 29: "Paul wishes to raise the minds of his followers that they may not flee, but bear all nobly. Therefore it is that he calls it a course (δρόμον) and shows it to be glorious from its being a race."

In commenting on I Cor. XI, 34: "If any man is hungry, let him eat at home . . . ." St. Chrysostom mentions the courses which Job ran in behalf of the needy and the naked. This follows his statement of Job, who said: "Jehovah gave, and Jehovah hath taken away; blessed be the name of Jehovah [Job. I, 21]." 61, 236, 34: "Job said these things, when he saw himself who had followed after all virtue in the last extremity. . . . He uttered no such word as it is likely that some of the weaker sort would have uttered. . . . 'Was it for this that after those many courses (δρόμους) run in behalf of the needy, the naked, the orphans, I might receive this recompense?'"

Peace is a race, as in Heb. XII, 14, 15: "Follow after peace with all men, and the sanctification without which no man shall see the Lord: looking carefully lest there be any man that falleth short (ὑστερῶν) of the grace of God . . . ." 63, 213, 5: "Many are the characteristic things of Christianity, but love and peace are the most characteristic of all. . . . Therefore Paul too says, 'Follow after peace with all men, and sanctification,' that is, purity (σεμνότητα),[1] 'without which no man shall see the Lord.'"

For those who have lived rightly death is a race toward the crowns, and so should not cause distress. 63, 802, 52: "As a farmer

---

[1]Properly, a disposition and conduct which creates respect or reverence: so specially, chastity.

seeing grain being dissolved (διαλυόμενον) does not therefore despair or become sad, so the just man, when he sees death placed before his eyes, does not become disturbed or distressed in mind like the crowd; for he knows that for those who have lived rightly death is a change for better things and a course (δρόμος) toward the crowns."

Death is also a speeding toward the crowns in 49, 183, 39. "What is able to throw a believer into sadness? Does not death seem the most insupportable of all things? Yet the expectation of this is so far from grieving him, that it makes him the more joyful; for he knows that the arrival of death is a release from labor and a speeding (δρόμος) toward the crowns and rewards (βραβεῖα) reserved for those who have contended (ἀγωνισαμένοις) in the race of piety and virtue." This idea is similarly expressed in 55, 230, 16 and 55, 281, 26.

The race of virtue is made easier to run because of Christ's coming which did away with sin. For this reason the goal is made more distant. The comment is on Rom. VI, 14: "For sin shall not have dominion over you: for ye are not under law, but under grace." 60, 487, 59: "Our body before Christ's coming was an easy prey to the assaults of sin; for a great swarm of passions entered. And for this cause it was not lightsome for running the race (δρόμον) of virtue. For there was no Spirit present to assist. But as some horse that answered not the rein,[1] it ran indeed, but made frequent slips (διημάρτανε), the law meanwhile announcing what was to be done and what not, yet not conveying into those in the race (ἀγωνιζομένοις) anything over and above exhortation by means of words. But when Christ had come, the effort became afterward more easy, and therefore we had a more distant goal (μείζονα τὰ σκάμματα) set us, in that the assistance given us was greater. Wherefore also Christ said, 'Except your righteousness shall exceed the righteousness of the scribes and Pharisees, ye shall in no wise enter into the kingdom of heaven [St. Matt. V, 20].'"

The same reason for the longer course occurs in the exegesis of Rom. VII, 6: "But now we have been discharged from the law. . . ." 60, 498, 58: "When Adam sinned and his body became liable to death and sufferings, it received also many physical losses, and the horse became less active and less obedient.[1] But Christ, when He came, made it more nimble for us through baptism, rousing it with the wing of the Spirit. And for this reason the marks (σκάμματα) for the race, which they of old time had to run, are not the same as ours,—since then the race was not so easy as it is now. For this

---

[1] Cf. Plato, Phaedrus 254.

reason He desires them to be clear not from murder only, as He did them of old time, but from anger also; nor is it adultery only from which He bids them keep clear, but even the unchaste look; and to be exempt not from false swearing only, but even from true. And with their friends He orders them to love their enemies also. And in all other duties He gives us a longer ground to run over (μακροτέρους τοὺς διαύλους) and, if we do not obey, threatens us with hell, so showing that the things in question are not matters of free-will offering for the combatants (ἀγωνιζομένων), as celibacy and poverty, but are binding upon us absolutely to fulfil."

The Christian should be thankful for the possibility of a greater race. Rom. VII, 25: "I thank God through Jesus Christ our Lord. . . ." 60, 512, 51: "Paul gives thanks for being delivered from the mortal body, that Christ has made us able to have a greater race (μείζονα δρόμον) set before us."

A free course is always desirable, and wherever found it is always commended. II Thess. III, 1: ". . . brethren, pray for us, that the word of the Lord may run and be glorified, even as also it is with you." 62, 489, 27: "The request is accompanied with commendation: 'Even as also it is with you.'"

The word of godliness will have a free course as in the Apostles' times, if the Christians will lead such a life so that the Greeks will not have reason to exercise censure. 57, 463, 35: "Let us show forth a new kind of life. Let us make earth heaven; let us hereby show the Greeks of how great blessings they are deprived. For when they behold in us good conversation, they will look upon the very face of the kingdom of heaven. Yea, when they see us gentle, pure from wrath, from evil desire, from envy, from covetousness, rightly fulfilling all our other duties, they will say, 'If the Christians are become angels here, what will they be after their departure hence?' . . . . Thus they too will be reformed, and the word of godliness will have free course (δραμεῖται) not less than in the Apostles' times. If we all should become teachers by our careful conduct, imagine how high our cause would be exalted. For not even a dead man raised so powerfully attracts the Greek, as a person practising self-denial (φιλοσοφῶν)."

Nothing should be a hindrance to any one in the race of virtue; and, as a matter of fact, there should be no reason for any excuse for not finishing the course. 57, 89, 21: "We should make neither place nor education nor forefathers' wickedness an excuse. Abraham had an ungodly father, but inherited not his wickedness; and Hezekiah, Ahaz: yet nevertheless he became dear to God. And Joseph, too, when in the midst of Egypt, adorned himself with the crowns of temperance; and the Three Children, no less in the midst of Babylon and of the palace, when a table like those at Sybaris was set before them, showed the highest self-denial; and Moses also in Egypt; and Paul in the whole world; but nothing was to any one of these a hindrance in the race (δρόμον) of virtue. Let us then apply ourselves to those toils which the cause of virtue requires. For thus shall we both attract to ourselves more favor from God and persuade Him to assist us in our struggles (συνεφάψασθαι τῶν ἀγώνων), and we shall obtain the eternal blessings."

The course can be run more easily only by decising superfluous wealth, as is indicated in St. Matt. XIX, 24: ". . . It is easier for a camel to go through a needle's eye, than for a rich man to enter into the kingdom of heaven." 58, 606, 2: "Christ affirmed it a work of God, that He might show that great grace is needed for him who must achieve this. At least, when the disciples were troubled, He said, 'With men this is impossible; but with God all things are possible [St. Matt. XIX, 26].' . . . . He said this, that, having considered the greatness of the good work, you should hasten (ἐπιπηδήσῃς) to it readily and, having besought God to assist (συνεφάψασθαι) you in these noble contests (ἄθλων), should attain (ἐπιτύχῃς) to life. . . . How is it possible for him who is once sunk in such lust of wealth to recover himself?—if he begins to empty himself of his possessions and to decise what is superfluous. For so shall he both advance further and run on his course (δραμεῖται) more easily afterward."

The Christian, like St. Paul, in running his race for the Church should not be actuated by vainglory. Gal. I, 14: "and I advanced in the Jews' religion beyond many of mine own age among my countrymen, being more exceedingly zealous for the traditions of my fathers." 61, 627, 4: "To obviate the notion that his persecution arose from passion, vainglory or enmity, he shows that he was actuated by a zealous admiration for the traditions of his fathers. This is his argument:—if my efforts against the Church sprang not from human motives, but from religious though mistaken zeal, why should I be actuated by vainglory, now that I am running (τρέχων) for the Church and have embraced the truth?"

Vainglory caused the Pharisee to fall behind in the running. 51, 311, 19: "The Pharisee publicly came forward as an accuser of the whole world and said that he himself was better than all living men. And yet even if he had set himself before ten only or five or two or one, not even was this endurable; but, as it was, he not only set himself before the whole world, but also accused all men. On this account he fell behind in the running (ὑστέρησε κατὰ τὸν δρόμον)."

One's conduct should be guarded, because of those who are spectators, as in Rom. XIV, 19: ". . . let us follow after things . . . whereby we may edify one another." 60, 641, 1: "Let us then watch our own conduct on all sides and afford to no one ever so little a handle (λαβήν). For this present life is a race-course (στάδιον), and we ought to have thousands of eyes on every side."

A priest has particular difficulty in his career toward God, as he must give considerable thought to the welfare of the female members of his church. 48, 684, 53: "Many are the circumstances in society which have the power to upset the balance of the soul and to hinder its career toward God (τὸν ἐπὶ Θεὸν διακόψαι δρόμον);[1] and first of all is his social intercourse with women. The female portion of the flock needs more particular forethought, because of its propensity to sins; and he must have a care of the moral health of these."

Closely allied with the idea of hindrances is that of things which render the course in vain. One must ever continue to be lowly-minded. 57, 36, 40: "Do not then mar your labors or cast away from you the fruits of your toils; nor run in vain, making frustrate all your labor after the many courses (τοὺς μυρίους διαύλους) which you have run."

If we do not assign the greater part to God, we run in vain, as is implied in Rom. IX, 16: ". . . it is not of him that willeth, nor of him that runneth, but of God that hath mercy." 63, 100, 15: "He did not then assert this, that we run in vain, but that, if we think the whole to be our own, if we do not assign the greater part to God, we run in vain. For God has willed that neither the whole should be His, lest He should appear to be crowning us without cause, nor again ours, lest we should fall away to pride."

Some interesting observations occur on the way of running the Christian race. It is not like that in the games, since even those who have fallen may yet be saved by conversion. 59, 96, 31: "In the games they whom all the spectators encourage are not those who have fallen and lie supine, but those who are exerting themselves and running still; of the others (since they would be doing what would be of no use and would not be able to raise by their encouragements men once for all severed from the victory) they cease to take any notice. But in this case some good may be expected, not only

---

[1] Another reading is τὸν ἐπ' εὐθείας διακόψαι.

of you who are sober, but even of those who have fallen, if they would but be converted."

The proof of a vigorous soul occurs in the case of those who rise again after having fallen into a grievous sin, just as the runner who after many victories suffers a loss, yet resumes the same course. David's slaying of Uriah to possess his wife is taken as a case in point. 57, 342, 16: "And how great a thing this is they best know, whosoever are fallen into grievous sins. For it is not so much a proof of a noble and vigorous soul to walk upright and to run all the way (for such a soul has the good hope going along with it, to anoint (ἀλείφουσαν) and rouse it, to nerve and render it more zealous), as after those innumerable crowns and so many trophies and victories, having undergone the utmost loss, to be able to resume the same course (ἐπιλαβέσθαι τῶν αὐτῶν δρόμων)."

An exhortation to prayer brings out the force of the word ἐκτενῶς: like a racer with every muscle "stretched out."[1] 51, 319, 15: "Are you in a calm? Then beseech God that this calm may continue settled for you. Have you seen a storm risen against you? Beseech God earnestly (ἐκτενῶς) to cause the billow to pass and to make a calm out of the storm."

Christ suffered all things and ran the entire course; so we must endure the whole contest and press on like St. Paul, as he says in Phil. III, 12: ". . . I press on, if so be that I may lay hold on that for which also I was laid hold on by Christ Jesus." 62, 267, 36: "By 'laying hold on,' Paul speaks of the prize (βραβεῖον), meaning the resurrection of the dead. . . . Christ suffered many things: He was spit upon, He was stricken, was scourged, at last He suffered what things He suffered [i.e., the Passion]. This is the entire course (στάδιον). Through all these things it is needful that men should endure the whole contest (ἄθλους) and so come to His resurrection and rise with glory. 'For not as yet,' says Paul, 'am I worthy,' but 'I press on, if so be that I may lay hold on.' My life is still one of contest (ἐναγώνιος), I am still far from the end, I am still distant from the prize (βραβείων), still I run, still I press on. And he said not, 'I run,' but 'I press on.' For you know with what eagerness a man pursues. He sees no one, he thrusts aside with great violence all who would interrupt his pursuit. He collects together his mind and sight and strength and soul and body, looking to nothing else than the prize (βραβεῖον). But if Paul, who so pursued, who had suffered so many things, yet says, 'If so be that I may lay hold on,' what should we say, who have relaxed our efforts?"

---

[1] *Cf.* Phil. III, 13: τοῖς ἔμπροσθεν ἐπεκτεινόμενος διώκω: the same metaphor.

He who loves Christ will incur dangers for Him, as does the athlete who runs for the greatest crowns. The exposition explains St. Matt. X, 37: "He that loveth father or mother more than me is not worthy of me. . . ." 60, 482, 20: "Christ bids us esteem our soul as second to the love of Him. . . . When we love any one warmly and really, we esteem love for him as a very great honor. . . . Let us then incur dangers for Him, as if running for the greatest crowns, and let us esteem neither poverty nor disease nor affront nor calumny nor death itself as heavy and burdensome, when it is for Him that we suffer these things."

St. Paul so ran as ever to keep his crown, although subject to the infirmity of human nature, as is shown in I Cor. II, 3: "And I was with you in weakness, and in fear, and in much trembling." 61, 49, 25: "This is no charge against Paul, for he was a man and subject to the infirmity of human nature. For this reason he must be admired; because being in fear, and not simply in 'fear,' but even in 'trembling,' at his perils, he so ran as ever to keep his crown."

The goal must never be lost from sight, as is expressed in Col. III, 3: ". . . your life is hid with Christ in God." 61, 508, 7: "And our prizes (ἔπαθλα) are there, and our race (δρόμοι) is for the crowns that are there."

The true Christian never ceases running, but always keeps his eye on the goal, reckoning how much of the race is still before him. The comment arises from Phil. III, 13, 14: "I. . . count not myself yet to have laid hold: but one thing I do, forgetting the things which are behind, and stretching forward to the things which are before, I press on toward the goal unto the prize of the high calling of God in Christ Jesus." 62, 270, 43: "Paul considers that he has not yet apprehended all virtue, as if one should speak of a runner. . . . For what made him reach forward to the things which are before was his forgetting the things that are behind. He then, who thinks that all is accomplished and that nothing is wanting to him for the perfecting of virtue, may cease running, as having apprehended all. But he, who thinks that he is still distant from the goal, will never cease running. . . . For the runner (δρομεύς) reckons not how many circuits (διαύλους) he has finished, but how many are left. We too should reckon, not how far we are advanced in virtue, but how much remains for us. . . . He who stretches forward is one who, though his feet are running, endeavors to outstrip them with the rest of his body, stretching himself towards the front and reaching out his hands, that he may accomplish somewhat more of the course (δρόμου). And this comes from great eagerness, from much warmth; thus the runner should run with great earnestness, without relaxation. As far as one who so runs differs from him who lies supine, so far Paul differs from us. He died daily, he was approved daily; there was no season, there was no time in which his course (δρόμος) advanced not. He wished not to take, but to snatch the prize (ἀρπάσαι τὸ βραβεῖον); for in this way we may take it. He who gives the prize stands on high; the prize is placed on high."

We should have no reason to despair as the contest is still on and the prize is still in suspense. This thought is inspired by Heb. IV, 16: "Let us therefore draw near with boldness unto the throne of grace, that we may receive mercy, and may find grace to help us in time of need." 63, 64, 29: "Now is the time of the gift; let no man despair of himself. . . . For still are the spectators, still is the contest (ἀγών), still is the prize (βραβεῖον) in suspense. Let us then be earnest. For even Paul says, 'I so run; as not uncertainly [I Cor. IX, 26].' There is need of running, and of running vehemently. He who runs a race sees none of those who meet him, whether passing through meadows or through dry places; he who runs looks not at the spectators, but at the prize (βραβεῖον). Whether they are rich or poor, whether one mocks him or praises him, whether one insults or casts stones at him or plunders his house, whether he sees children or wife or anything whatever, he is occupied in one thing alone, in running, in gaining the prize (βραβεῖον). He who runs never stands still, since, even if he slackens a little, he has lost the whole. He who runs not only slackens nothing before the end, but then even especially strains (ἐπιτείνει) his speed. This have I spoken for those who say: 'In our younger days we used discipline (ἠσκήσαμεν), in our younger days we fasted, now we are grown old.' Now most of all it behooves you to make your carefulness more intense. Do not enumerate to me the old things especially done well; be now youthful and vigorous. For he who runs this bodily race, when gray hairs have overtaken him, probably is not able to run as he did before: for the whole contest (τὸ πᾶν τοῦ ἀγῶνος) depends on the body; but you,—wherefore do you lessen your speed? For in this race there is need of a soul, a soul thoroughly awakened: and the soul is rather strengthened in old age; then is it in its full vigor, then is it in its pride."

The nearness of the prize should rouse the Christian runner the more, as is suggested by Rom. XIII, 11: "And this, knowing the season, that already it is time for you to awake out of sleep: for now is salvation nearer to us than when we first believed." 60, 622,

52: "The nearer the prize (βραβεῖον) is, the more wide awake (διεγείρεσθαι) ought we to be for the contest (ἀγῶνας), since even the racers (δρομεῖς) do this, when they are upon the end of the course (δρόμου) and about to receive the prize, then they rouse themselves (διανίστανται) the more. This is why he said, 'Now is our salvation nearer than when we believed.'" Exertion at the end of the race occurs also in 53, 273, 28 and 55, 519, 14.

The spectators cheer on those who are near upon gaining the victory; so St. Paul has good reason for what he says in Col. I, 9: "For this cause we also, since the day we heard it, do not cease to pray for you." 62, 309, 17: "Because we have heard of your faith and love, . . . we are hopeful to ask for future blessings also. For as in the games (ἀγῶσιν) we cheer on (ἐγείρομεν) those most who are near upon gaining the victory, just so does Paul also most exhort those who have achieved the greater part."

The Christian, like the racer, must finish all the laps, else he has lost all. Exhorting to good works, St. Chrysostom says (62, 180, 42): "It is not once we have to please God, but constantly. For if the racer (ὁ τρέχων) after running ten heats (διαύλους) leaves the last one (τὸν ὕστερον) undone, he has lost all; so we also, if we begin with good works and afterward faint, have lost all."

The Christian must run to the end, to show himself unblameable to win the prize. The comment is on I Cor. IX, 24: "Know ye not that they that run in a race run all, but one receiveth the prize?. . . ." 61, 189, 7: "Paul sets forth the exceeding diligence which it is our duty to use. For as there, though many descend into the course (στάδιον), not many are crowned, but this befalls one only; and it is not enough to descend into the contest or anoint one's self and wrestle; so likewise here it is not sufficient to believe and contend (ἀγωνίσασθαι) in any way; but unless we so run that we may show ourselves unblameable and come near the prize (βραβείου), it will profit us nothing."

St. Paul exhorts (61, 263, 17) to proper emulation. Rom. XI, 14: "if by any means I may provoke to jealousy them that are my flesh, and may save some of them." This sort of emulation will enable us to obtain the crowns. Ib. 264, 33: "Let us expel from within us the fever of envy, which is more grievous than any gangrene, that, having regained spiritual strength, we may both finish (διανύσωμεν) the present course (ἀγῶνα) and obtain the future crowns."

The Christian race can be run with ease. The Christian runner need not run when he is lame, as is expressed in Heb. XII, 13: "and make straight paths for your feet, that that which is lame be not turned out of the way, but rather be healed." 63, 209, 47: "He speaks as to runners (δρομεῖς); . . . for he, who runs when he is lame, galls the sore place. Do you see that it is in our power to be healed thoroughly?"

The Holy Spirit enables us to run the race of virtue for the reason given in Rom. VIII, 10: "And if Christ is in you, the body is dead because of sin; but the spirit is life because of righteousness." 60, 519, 16: "Christ's indwelling enables us to run with ease the race of virtue. For he does not say so little as that the body is henceforward inactive for sin, but that it is even dead, so magnifying the ease of the race. For such an one without troubles and labors gains the crown."

We need not faint in the course of the race, because Christ's joy will remain in us, as is stated in St. John XV, 11: "These things have I spoken unto you, that my joy may be in you, and that your joy may be made full ('fulfilled,' πληρωθῇ)." 59, 413, 51: "All good things have their reward, when they arrive at their proper end. . . . Great is the calamity in the case of those souls which fall back when near the end of their labors and faint in the midst of the struggles (ἐν μέσοις ἐκλυόμεναι τοῖς ἀγῶσι). Wherefore Paul said that 'glory and honor' and peace should meet those who ran their course 'by patience in well-doing [Rom. II, 7].' . . . . Since the disciples rejoiced in Him and since the sudden coming of the Passion was likely to cut short their pleasure, He said: 'These things have I spoken unto you, that my joy may remain in you, and that your joy may be made full;' that is, 'that you may not be separated from me, that you may not cut short your course (δρόμον).'"

Earthly things cannot bind him who runs in heaven, as is elaborated on Col. IV, 3: ". . . to speak the mystery of Christ, for which I am also in bonds." 62, 369, 59: "Paul, the teacher of the world, who had ascended into the third heaven, who had heard the unspeakable words, was bound. But then was his course (δρόμος) the swifter. He who was bound, was now loosed; for he indeed was doing what he would. Do you think that he is a fleshly runner? Does he strive (ἀγωνίζεται) in our race-course (σταδίῳ)? His course of life is in heaven; him who runs in heaven things on earth can not bind or hold. See you not this sun? Enclose its beams with fetters! Stay it from its course! You can not. Then you can not Paul!"

It seems fitting to close this chapter with two of St. Chrysostom's comments on St. Paul's notable declaration about having finished the course. The first occurs in 52, 413, 18, where corporeal and spiritual beauty are contrasted, showing that the Christian race may be finished, so that the graceless soul like that of St. Paul can become full of grace. "For as in the case of the body I was saying that he who is ungraceful cannot become graceful, so in the case of the soul I say the contrary, that the graceless soul can become full of grace. For what was more graceless than the soul of Paul, when he was a blasphemer and insulter: what more full of grace when he said [II Tim. IV, 7]: 'I have fought the good fight, I have finished the course, I have kept the faith'?"

The second statement (62, 652, 17) is based on the verse itself. "Often, when I have taken the Apostle into my hands, and have considered this passage, I have been at a loss to understand why Paul here speaks so loftily: 'I have fought the good fight (τὸν ἀγῶνα τὸν καλὸν ἠγώνισμαι).' But now by the grace of God I seem to have discovered it. For what purpose then does he speak thus? He is desirous to console the despondency of his disciple, and therefore bids him be of good cheer, since he is going to his crown, having finished all his work and obtained a glorious end. . . . 'The good fight (τὸν ἀγῶνα τὸν καλόν),' he says, 'therefore do you engage in it.' But is that a good fight (ἀγών), where there are imprisonment, chains and death? Yea, he says; for it is fought in the cause of Christ, and great crowns are won in it. 'The good fight'! There is none other worthier than this contest (ἀγῶνος). This crown is without end. This is not of olive-leaves (κοτίνων). It has not a human umpire (ἄνθρωπον ἀγωνοθέτην). It has not men for spectators. The theatre is crowded with angels. There men labor many days suffering hardships; and for one hour they receive the crown, and immediately all the pleasure vanishes. But here, far otherwise, it continues forever in brightness, glory and honor. Henceforth we ought to rejoice. For I am entering on my rest, I am leaving the race (ἐξέρχομαι τὸ στάδιον). 'I have finished the course (τὸν δρόμον τετέλεκα).' For it behooves us both to contend (ἀγωνίζεσθαι) and to run; to contend, by enduring afflictions firmly, and to run, not vainly, but to some good end. It is truly a good fight (ἀγών), not only delighting, but benefiting the spectator; and the race does not end in nothing. It is not a mere display of strength and of rivalry. It raises all to heaven. This race which Paul ran upon earth is brighter than that which the sun runs in heaven."

3. WRESTLING[1]

We may judge from the numerous references that, of all the contests, wrestling was the one which was most highly held in regard, because of the skill and the strength involved therein. It was not a brutal sight to behold as was boxing; while for endurance, skill and strength, it no doubt was esteemed greater than running. A great wrestler was always regarded with the most earnest attention. This is shown in the preface to the *Homiliae in S. Johannem*, 59, 23, 1: "They who are spectators of the games, when they have learned that a distinguished athlete and winner of crowns (γενναῖον ἀθλητὴν καὶ τὴν στεφανίτην) is come from any quarter, run all together to view his wrestling (παλαίσματα) and all his skill and strength (τὴν τέχνην καὶ τὴν ἰσχύν); and you may see the whole theatre of many myriads, all there straining their eyes both of body and of mind, that nothing of what is done may escape them. . . . If, in the case of athletes, people assist with such earnest attention, what zeal, what earnestness ought you in reason to display when a man [St. John] speaks from heaven and utters a voice plainer than thunder?"

There is a greater pleasure in beholding spiritual wrestlings than worldly. These may be witnessed in the Bible, where we may learn how to wrestle and escape from the devil. 59, 188, 3: "Which is sweeter, tell me, which more marvellous: to see a man wrestling with a man or a man boxing with a devil; a body closing with (συμπλεκόμενον) an incorporeal power, and him who is of your race vic-

---

[1]Wrestling was perhaps the most popular of all sports among the Greeks and Romans. Metaphors on wrestling abound in both literatures, and in art the contests of Heracles and Theseus are constantly represented as wrestling-matches. The Greeks distinguished between upright-wrestling, in which the object was to throw the opponent, and ground-wrestling. The latter was admitted only in the *pancratium*; the former alone was allowed in the *pentathlon* and in wrestling-competitions. The victor was he who threw his opponent three times. It was a fair fall, if a wrestler touched the ground with any part of his body, hip, back or shoulder. If he fell or sank on his knee, it probably did not count as a fall; nor did it count, if both wrestlers fell together. For this reason both bouts in the match between Ajax and Odysseus recorded in the *Iliad* (Bk. XXIII) counted nothing. Tripping was freely used, but leg-holds from the nature of the competition were too risky to be much employed. The methods of the Greek wrestler were as varied as those of the present day. In competitions the ties were drawn by lots, and the fortunate drawer of a bye had a great advantage in the next round. The Homeric wrestler wore a loin-cloth, but in historic times nothing was worn. The wrestler first oiled his body and rubbed it with fine sand. Hence a wrestler who had a "walk-over" was said to have won ἀκονιτί.

torious? On these wrestlings let us look: by these, which also it is seemly and profitable to imitate (and imitating which), we may be crowned, but not by those in which emulation brings shame to him who imitates them. If you behold the one kind of wrestling, you behold it with devils; the other, with angels and archangels and the Lord of archangels. Say now, if you were allowed to sit with governors and kings and to see and enjoy the spectacle, would you not deem it a very great honor? And here when you are a spectator in company with the King of angels, when you see the devil grasped by the middle of the back, striving much to have the better, but powerless, do you not run and pursue after such a sight as this? 'And how can this be?' says some one;—if you keep the Bible in your hands. For in it you shall see the lists and the long races and his grasps and. the skill ($\sigma\kappa\acute{\alpha}\mu\mu\alpha\tau\alpha$, $\mu\alpha\kappa\rho o\grave{\upsilon}s$ $\delta\iota\alpha\acute{\upsilon}\lambda o\upsilon s$, $\lambda\alpha\beta\acute{\alpha}s$, $\tau\acute{\epsilon}\chi\nu\eta\nu$) of the righteous one. For by beholding these things you yourself shall learn also how to wrestle and shall escape clear of devils. . . . God grant that you may be deemed worthy to enjoy the spiritual spectacle and the glory which is to come!"

That the bad exists to give wrestlings to the good arises from St. Matt. XXVI, 24: ". . . but woe unto that man through whom the Son of man is betrayed! good were it for that man if he had not been born." 58, 733, 1: "Some one will say, 'And if it had been good if he had never been born, wherefore did He suffer both this man and all the wicked to come into the world?' . . . If you still demand reasons, we would say this, that the good are more admired for being among the bad, because their long-suffering and great self-command is then most shown. But you take away the occasion of their wrestlings ($\pi\alpha\lambda\alpha\iota\sigma\mu\acute{\alpha}\tau\omega\nu$) and conflicts ($\dot{\alpha}\gamma\acute{\omega}\nu\omega\nu$) by saying these things."

Cain would have attained a glorious crown, if he had conquered Abel living. 60, 449, 51: "If you would be a conqueror over your brother, kill not, destroy not, but let him abide still, that the material for the struggle ($\pi\alpha\lambda\alpha\iota\sigma\mu\acute{\alpha}\tau\omega\nu$) may be preserved, and conquer him living. For in this way your crown would have been a glorious one ($\lambda\alpha\mu\pi\rho\acute{o}s$)."

The loss of a wife may be only to call one to a nobler conflict. 61, 362, 44: "Even if you shall lose a wife, give thanks [Job. I, 21: 'Jehovah gave, and Jehovah hath taken away']. Perhaps God's will is to lead you to continence. He calls you to a nobler field of conflict ($\mu\epsilon\acute{\iota}\zeta o\nu\alpha$ $\sigma\kappa\acute{\alpha}\mu\mu\alpha\tau\alpha$). He was pleased to set you free from this bond. If we thus command ourselves, we shall both gain the joy of this life and obtain the crowns which are to come."

Women as well as men are admitted to the contest of Christian wrestling. 63, 488, 23: "In the contests (παλαισμάτων) of religion the stadium is common to both sexes. There the women strip and are not cast forth from the contest (ἀγῶνος), but contend and are crowned and proclaimed and obtain prizes and rewards (ἔπαθλα καὶ βραβεῖα) and crowns of excellence."

Wrestlings are decided not by bodily constitution, but by mental choice. 57, 87, 48: "The war against the devil and his powers is common to women and men, and in no respect does the delicacy of their nature become an impediment in such conflicts, for not by bodily constitution, but by mental choice, are these struggles (παλαί-σματα) decided. Wherefore women in many cases have actually been more forward in the contest (ἠγωνίσαντο) than men and have erected more brilliant trophies."

Two kinds of wrestling-contests are mentioned: the priesthood and virginity. The priesthood is a contest in protecting the flock by wrestling "against the principalities, against the powers, against the world-rulers of this darkness, against the spiritual hosts of wickedness in the heavenly places (Eph. VI, 12)." 48, 633, 22: "Let the distinction between the pastor and his charge be as great as that between rational man and irrational creatures, not to say even greater, inasmuch as the risk is concerned with things of far greater importance. He indeed who has lost sheep, through either the ravages of wolves or the attacks of robbers or murrain or any other disaster befalling them, may perhaps obtain some indulgence from the owner of the flock (and even if the latter should demand satisfaction, the penalty would be only a matter of money); but he who has human beings intrusted to him, the rational flock of Christ, incurs a penalty in the first place for the loss of the sheep, which goes beyond material things and touches his own life, and in the second place he must carry on a far greater and more difficult contest (ἀγῶνα). For he has not to contend with wolves or to dread robbers or to consider how he may avert pestilence from the flock. With whom then has he to fight? With whom has he to wrestle? Listen to the words of the blessed Paul, 'Our wrestling is not against flesh and blood, but against the principalities, etc.'"

Virginity, the second kind of wrestling-contest, should always be maintained when once it has been vowed. The comment is on I Cor. VII, 9: ". . . if they have not continency, let them marry . . . ." 48, 561, 7: "No one says to an athlete after he has thrown off his cloak and been anointed and gone into the stadium and sprinkled himself with dust: 'Go away and flee from your antagonist (ἀνταγωνιστήν).'

But it is necessary that one of the two should be left, either crowned or, having fallen, gone away in shame. In the *palaestra* where training (γυμνασία) is with friends as opponents, one has his choice of laboring or not laboring; but when his name is registered on the list and the spectators are assembled and the judge (ἀγωνοθέτης) is present and the antagonist is introduced and placed opposite him, the laws of the contests [games] have taken away his choice ('power,' ἐξουσίαν). Just so with the maiden, while she is consulting as to whether she should marry or not, marriage is safe; but when she has made her choice and her name is registered, she brings herself into the stadium. Who will then dare, when the angels are looking on from above and Christ is the judge (ἀγωνοθετοῦντος) and the devil is angry and gnashing his teeth and engaging in the wrestling-combat and is seized by the middle, who will dare to come into the midst and say: 'Flee from the opponent, keep away from his grasp, do not trip up your antagonist, but yield the victory to him?'"

Virginity is a wrestling for which not even Moses or Abraham dared to strip. St. Chrysostom in writing to Olympias tells how great virginity is and quotes St. Matt. XIX, 12: "He that is able to receive it, let him receive it." 52, 563, 18: "Great is the difficulty of these wrestlings (παλαισμάτων) and the sweat of the contests. . . . Even Moses, chief of the prophets and the true friend of God, who gave evidence of countless brilliant contests, was not able to look on this contest. . . . And Abraham, who brought himself to the point of enduring the contest of sacrificing his only son, did not dare to strip for the contest of virginity (ἀγῶνας τῆς παρθενίας); but he feared this contest (σκάμματα) and embraced the solace of marriage."

We now come to the main part of this chapter,—the manner and means of engaging in the wrestling-contest itself. First of all, the wrestler must be in the best condition. Both soul and body must be fed with frugality; in fact, soul and body are like charioteer and horse, and a plump body is as disadvantageous to the soul in wrestling as a plump horse is to the charioteer in a chariot-race. 60, 208, 44: "Now is the season for contest (ἀγῶνος); and do you sit enjoying yourself? . . . . 'Our wrestling is not against flesh and blood [Eph. VI, 12];' and are you fattening yourself when about to wrestle? The adversary (ἀντίπαλος) stands grinding his teeth (τρίζων τοὺς ὀδόντας); and are you giving a loose to jollity and devoting yourself to the table? . . . . If none other, let the wrestlers (ἀθληταί) teach you, that the more spare (ἰσχνότερον) the body is, the stronger (ἰσχυρότερον) it is: and then also the soul is more vigorous. In fact, it is like charioteer and horse. But there you see, just as in the case of men giving themselves to luxury and making themselves plump, so the plump horses are unwieldy (δυσκινήτους) and give the driver much ado. One may think one's self well-off (ἀγαπητόν), even with a horse obedient to the rein and well-limbed, to be able to carry off the prize (βραβεῖον); but when the driver (ἡνίοχος) is forced to drag the horse along and when the horse falls, though he goads him ever so much, he cannot make him get up; though he is ever so skillful himself, he will be deprived of the victory. Then let us not endure to see our soul wronged because of the body, but let us make the soul itself more clear-sighted and its wing light. Let us feed it with frugality, feeding the body only so much that it may be healthy, that it may be vigorous, that it may rejoice and not be in pain: that, having in this sort well ordered our concerns, we may be enabled to lay hold upon the highest virtue."

The soul of the righteous is youthful and ever ready for any struggle. 60, 480, 54: "The soul of the sinner is decayed and totters with many sins; . . . not so those of the righteous, for they are youthful and well-favored and in the very prime of life throughout, ever ready for any fight or struggle (πάλην)."

That he who truly contends always struggles and knows the laws of the contest is drawn from Jer. XIV, 14: ". . . the prophets prophesy lies in my name . . . ." 64, 897, 44: "The Apostle Paul gives the solution in making a distinction between what is true and false. . . . 'No one is crowned, except he have contended lawfully [II Tim. II, 5].' And he who truly contends (ἀθλῶν) always struggles (ἀγωνίζεται) against opponents (ἀντιπάλους) and must know these laws of a spiritual contest (πάλης). And the greater is his love toward God, the more contests (ἀγώνων) are there which do not conquer this [love]: and the highest force of incorporeal and divine power is shown."

We should not be discouraged if we fall, because it is still in our power to recover ourselves and attain achievements of good works. 60, 187, 41: "If the newly-baptized one happens to depart immediately from this life, those that are left are not cheated of the prize, but have received a greater gift, because they have received a set time for winning distinction which the other one did not have. . . . The other goes his way, having only the reward of his faith; you stand in the course (σταδίῳ), both able to obtain an abundant recompense for your works and to show yourself as much more glorious than he, as the sun is than the smallest star. . . . It is in your power to contend afresh. Have you been thrown (κατεβλήθης)? Have you taken grievous hurt? Stand up, recover yourself (ἀνάκτησαι): you are still in the course (σταδίῳ), the meeting (θέατρον) is not yet concluded. Do you not see how many who have been thrown in the wrestling (καταπαλαισθέντες) have afterward resumed the combat? Only do not willingly come by your fall."

Noble wrestlers not only need no consolation themselves, but even become a consolation to others. Heb. X, 32, 34: ". . . ye endured a great conflict (ἄθλησιν) of sufferings . . . . For ye both had compassion on them that were in bonds. . . ." 63, 149, 5: "He did not say 'temptations' but 'fight (ἄθλησιν),' which is an expression of commendation and of very great praise. . . . You did not account 'bonds' to be bonds; but as noble wrestlers (ἀθληταί) so stood you: for not only you needed no consolation in your own distress, but even became a consolation to others."

The wrestler struggles to the point where refreshment is welcome. II Tim. I, 16: ". . . for he [Onesiphorus] oft refreshed me. . . ." 62, 616, 3: "Like a wearied wrestler (ἀθλητήν) overcome by heat (αὐχμοῦ, 'drought') and tribulations, Onesiphorus refreshed and strengthened him [St. Paul]."

The Christian Wrestler is not conscious of his suffering when he knows that it is for God. 57, 398, 7: "I admire the Three Children, because they dared the furnace, because they withstood the tyrant. But hear what they say, 'We serve not thy gods, nor worship the image which thou hast set up [Dan. III, 18],'—a thing which was the greatest encouragement to them, to know of a certainty that for God they were suffering all whatsoever they suffered. But this man [Job] knew not that it was all conflicts (ἀγωνίσματα) and a wrestling (πάλη); for if he had known it, he would not have felt what was happening."

We are exhorted to wrestle while the contest of the present life is still in progress. This is expressed in commenting on I Cor. X, 12: "Wherefore let him that thinketh he standeth take heed lest he fall." 61, 195, 27: "For if in the present life we exhibit even an ordinary diligence, we shall gain the greatest rewards; but if we depart having become nothing better here, even though we repent ever so earnestly there, it will do us no good. For it was our duty to strive (ἀγωνίσασθαι) while yet remaining within the lists (σκαμμάτων), not to lament idly and weep, after the assembly (θέατρον) was concluded." In 53, 163, 17 Cain is condemned for not having repented, while he had the opportunity for wrestling.

We must wrestle always, as in I Cor. IV, 11: "Even unto this present hour we both hunger, and thirst, and are naked, and are buffeted . . . ." 61, 108, 22: "The life of Christians must be such as this, and not merely for a day or two. For though the wrestler, who is victorious in a single contest only, is crowned, he is not crowned again, if he suffers a fall (καταπεσών)."

God wills that His champion should wrestle to death. St. Matt. XVI, 24: "Then said Jesus unto his disciples, If any man would come after me, let him deny himself, and take up his cross, and follow me." 58, 542, 20: "He says how far one ought to renounce one's self: that is, to death, and that a reproachful death. 'Yea,' says he, 'bear about this death continually and day by day be ready for slaughter. For since many have indeed contemned riches and pleasure and glory, but death they despised not, but feared dangers, I,' says He, 'will that My champion (ἀγωνιστήν) should wrestle even to blood and that his wrestling-grounds (σκάμματα) should reach to slaughter.'"

Victorious wrestlers are eager to maintain their reputation and add another victory to their credit. 53, 273, 31: "After countless wrestlings and victories, when wrestlers are wrestling for the crown, they display a greater exertion, that they may thus depart from the contest with the crown." The same statement is also found in 55, 519, 16.

The experienced wrestler should guard against becoming careless. 56, 115, 5: "For one who has fallen in the beginning we all make allowance for his lack of experience; but one can not easily claim pardon or defence for the one who has been overthrown after many contests, for then the fall (πτῶμα) seems to result from carelessness and indifference."

The true wrestler never chooses to be in repose. St. Chrysostom is speaking to those who have a mad desire for riches. 58, 686, 28: "If we should taste as we ought of spiritual fruits, we shall thenceforth not even account the things present to be anything, being seized by the desire of the things to come as with some most noble intoxication. . . . Thus Paul suffers hunger and is held in honor more than when he ate. Forasmuch as a wrestler (ἀθλητής) also, when striving (ἀγωνιζόμενος) and winning crowns, would not choose to surrender and to be in repose (ῥᾳστώνῃ)."

Old age has its special period of usefulness in the cause of virtue. 63, 517, 6: "When the farmer is old, he retires from active work; . . . while the teacher in the church then contends (ἀγωνιεῖται) especially and lays hold on (ἅψεται) words and sets forth his teaching and tries to improve the people's morals. The blessed Abraham entered upon his greatest contest (ἆθλον) at this time of life. . . .

And Paul, the teacher of the world, in deepest old age stripped for those marvellous contests (ἀγῶνας) and endured chain and prison in an aged body with much constancy."

If we depart this life still wrestling, we are conquerors. 62, 162, 2: "Paul was not slothful, so Satan did not prevail over him in any instance. But in our own case, it is matter for contentment that we should be so much as able to wrestle. For the Romans indeed this is not what he asks, but what? 'He [God] shall bruise Satan under your feet shortly [Rom. XVI, 20].' And for these [Ephesians] he thus prays, 'Unto him that is able to do exceeding abundantly above all that we ask or think [Eph. III, 20].' He who wrestles is still held fast, but it is enough for him that he has not fallen. When we depart hence, then, and not till then, will the glorious victory be achieved. For instance, take the case of some evil lust. The extraordinary thing would be, not even to entertain it, but to stifle it. If, however, this is not possible, then though we may have to wrestle with it and retain it to the last, yet, if we depart still wrestling, we are conquerors. For the case is not the same here as it is with wrestlers (ἀθλητῶν): for there, if you throw not your antagonist, you have not conquered; but here, if you are not thrown, you have conquered; if you are not thrown, you have thrown him,—and with reason, because there both strive for the victory, and, when the one is thrown, the other is crowned; here, however, it is not thus, but the devil is striving for our defeat: when then I strip him of that upon which he is bent, I am conqueror. For it is not to overthrow us, but to make us share his overthrow, that he is eager. Already then am I conqueror, for he is already cast down and in a state of ruin; and his victory consists not in being himself crowned, but in effecting my ruin: so that, though I overthrow him not, yet if I am not overthrown, I have conquered."

A last struggle may enable the wrestler to recover all his former defeats. Is. I, 18: ". . . though your sins be as scarlet, they shall be as white as snow . . . ." 60, 580, 58: "When it is God that promises, doubt not, but do those things whereby you may draw to you these promises. . . . Hitherto the arena (θέατρον) is not concluded for you, but you are standing within the line (σκάμματος) and you are able even by a struggle at the last (ἐσχάτης πάλης) to recover (ἀναπαλαῖσαι, 'retrieve by contest') all your defeats."

We are not as successful in our wrestling as the early Christians for the reason given in the comment on Acts II, 37: "Now when they heard this, they were pricked in their heart, and said unto Peter and the rest of the apostles, Brethren, what shall we do?" 60, 68, 19:

"They entered into the contest (ἀγῶνα) at once and took off the coat; whereas we do enter, but we intend to do our wrestling wearing our coat. This is why our antagonist has so little trouble, for we get entangled in our own movements and are continually thrown. We do precisely the same as he, who, seeing a professed wrestler (ἄνδρα ἀθλητήν) covered with dust (κεκονιμένον),[1] tanned (μέλανα), stripped, clotted with dirt from sand and sun, and running down with sweat and oil and dirt, himself, smelling of perfumes, should put on his silken garments, his gold shoes, his robe hanging down to his heels, his golden trinkets on his head, and so descend into the wrestling-place and grapple with him. Such an one will not only be impeded, but, concerned with the sole idea of not staining or rending his fine clothes, will also tumble at the very first onset and withal will suffer that which he chiefly dreaded, the damage of his fond delights. The time for the contest (ἀγῶνος) is come, and are you putting on your silks? It is the time of exercise (γυμνασίας), the hour of the race (σταδίου), and are you adorning yourself as for a procession?"

When seized with Christ's flame maidens shame the men in stripping themselves of riches and rushing into the contest. 62, 98, 3: "Damsels not yet twenty years old, who have spent their whole time in inner chambers and in a delicate and effeminate mode of life in inner chambers full of sweet ointments and perfumes, reclining on soft couches, themselves soft in their nature, and rendered yet more tender by their over-indulgence, who all the day long have had no other business than to adorn themselves, to wear jewels and to enjoy every luxury, who never waited on themselves, but had numerous handmaids standing beside them, who wore soft raiment softer than their skin, fine linen and delicate, who revelled continually in roses and such like sweet odors,—yea, these very ones, in a moment, seized with Christ's flame, have put off all that indolence and even their very nature, have forgotten their delicacy and youth and, like so many noble wrestlers (ἀθληταὶ γενναῖοι), have stripped themselves of that soft clothing and rushed into the midst of the contest (εἰς μέσους τοὺς ἀγῶνας)."

There should be no idle words in our present contest. Eph. V, 4: ". . . nor foolish talking, or jesting, which are not befitting . . . ." 62, 118, 22: "Let there not be one idle word, for the present is no season of loose merriment. What wrestler (ἀθλητής) on entering the stadium neglects the struggle (ἀγωνίαν) with his adversary and utters witticisms (ἀστεῖα)?"

---

[1]Cf. Lucian, Anacharsis 3: κεκονιμένοι.

Athletes are influenced by the kind of spectators which they have. Speaking of the scribes and Pharisees Christ says, ". . . all their works they do to be seen of men . . . [St. Matt. XXIII, 5]." 58, 669, 6: "These things He says, accusing them in respect of vainglory, which kind of thing was their ruin. This drew them off from God, this caused them to strive (ἀγωνίζεσθαι) before other spectators (ἐν ἑτέρῳ θεάτρῳ) and ruined them. For whatever kind of spectators any one may have, since it has become his study to please these, such also are the contests (ἀγῶνας) which he exhibits. And he who wrestles (παλαίων) among the noble (ἐν γενναίοις), such also are the conflicts (ἀγωνίσματα) which he takes in hand; but he among the cold and supine, himself also becomes more remiss (ῥᾳθυμότερος). For instance, has any one a beholder who delights in ridicule? He himself, too, becomes a mover of ridicule, that he may delight the spectator. Has another one who is earnest-minded and practises self-control (φιλοσοφοῦντα)? He endeavors himself to be such as he is, since such is the disposition of him who praises him."

The hypocrites do not imitate those who wrestle in the Olympic games. St. Matt. VI, 16: ". . . when ye fast, be not, as the hypocrites, of a sad countenance: for they disfigure their faces, that they may be seen of men to fast . . . ." 57, 288, 12: "The hypocrites fast as well as we, but God does not suffer us to go away unrewarded, as they do. Nay, they [the hypocrites] will not so much as imitate those who wrestle in the Olympic games, who, although so great a multitude is sitting there and so many princes (ἀρχόντων), desire to please but one, even him who adjudges (βραβεύοντι) the victory among them,—and this, though he is much their inferior. But you, though you have a twofold motive for displaying the victory to Him: first, that He is the person to adjudge (βραβεύοντα) it, and second, that He is beyond comparison superior to all who are sitting in the theatre,—you are displaying it to others, who, so far from profiting, do privately work you the greatest harm."

Vanity deprives the wrestler of his reward. 60, 570, 64: "God remembers your well-doings even after this life, but man only for the present. And when you have spectators assembled in heaven, you are gathering together spectators upon earth. And where the wrestler struggles, there he would be honored; but you, while your wrestling is above, are anxious to gain a crown below."

Our wrestlings are worthy even of angelic contemplation. I Cor. IV, 9: ". . . for we are made a spectacle unto the world, both to angels and men." 61, 99, 46: "We do not suffer these things in a small part of the world, but everywhere and before all. Our wrestlings (παλαίσματα) are such as to be worthy even of angelic contemplation. .... For not with men only is our wrestling, but also with incorporeal powers. Therefore also a mighty theatre is set. . . . Not only are angels looking on, but, even more than they, He who presides over the spectacle (ἀγωνοθέτης)."

It is Satan's manner of wrestling to keep the temptation of riches for the last. 57, 212, 50: "In Christ's case Satan kept the temptation of riches for the last, as being of more force than the rest. For in fact this is the manner of his wrestling (τῆς πάλης ὁ νόμος), to apply those things last which seem more likely to overthrow (ὑποσκελίζειν). And this sort of thing he did with respect to Job likewise."

Wealth and vainglory give the devil a hold. 62, 162, 28: "We may obtain a glorious victory over the devil as Paul did, by regarding the things of this present world as nothing. Let us imitate him and strive to become above them and nowhere to give him a hold (λαβήν) upon us. Wealth, possessions and vainglory give him a hold. And often indeed this has aroused him and often exasperated him. But what need is there of wrestling (πάλης)? What need of engaging with (συμπλοκῆς) him? He who is engaged in the act of wrestling has the issue in uncertainty, whether he may not himself be defeated. Whereas he that tramples him underfoot has the victory certain."

Benevolence strengthens the soul as oil does the body, making it invincible to the devil. St. Matt. XIX, 27: "Then answered Peter and said unto him, Lo, we have left all, and followed thee; what then shall we have?" 58, 615, 42: "For oil (ἔλαιον) does not so strengthen a body, as benevolence at once strengthens a soul and makes it invincible (ἀχείρωτον) to all and impregnable (ἀνάλωτον) to the devil. For wheresoever he may seize us, his hold then slips (διολισθαίνει), this oil not suffering his grasp (λαβάς) to fix on (ἐνιζάνειν) our back. With this oil therefore let us anoint ourselves (ἀλείφωμεν) continually. For it is the cause of health and a supply of light and a source of cheerfulness."

St. Paul anoints the wrestler with hope, which makes the soul courageous and gives him a firm footing. Rom. XII, 12: "rejoicing in hope; patient in tribulation; continuing steadfastly in prayer." 60, 605, 61: "When Paul had required the expenditure of money and labor of the person and ruling and zeal and teaching and other laborious occupations, he again anointed (ἀλείφει) the wrestler (ἀθλητήν) with love, with the Spirit, through hope. For there is nothing which makes the soul so courageous and venturesome for anything as a good hope. . . . You see how in every way he gives the wrestler (ἀθλητήν) firm footing and shows that the injunctions are perfectly easy."

The devil used craftiness in beginning his wrestlings with Christ, 57, 210, 30. "After He hungered, it is said, 'The tempter came and said unto him, If thou art the Son of God, command that these stones become bread [St. Matt. IV, 3]'. . . . He said not, 'because thou art hungry,' but 'if thou art the Son of God;' thinking to cheat Him with his compliments. . . . Flattering Him craftily, he makes mention of His dignity only. . . . Mark the craft of that wicked demon and whence he begins his wrestlings (παλαισμάτων) and how he forgets not his proper art."

The devil, having cast Adam from paradise through a woman, reserved Job's wife till the last in the hope of tripping him. Job II, 9: "Then said his wife unto him, Dost thou still hold fast thine integrity? renounce God, and die." 64, 557, 22: "But he, when he came out from the last contest (ἀγῶνος), again was wreathed with other crowns from those words to his wife. For the devil had reserved his wife until the last to try him, when everything else that he had was gone, children and property and health of body. Having cast Adam from paradise through a woman he had hoped to trip up (ὑποσκελίσαι) Job much easier on his dunghill."

The same method of the devil is also given in 61, 237, 6. "The devil suffers Job's wife to be silent and quiet as she looks on the combatant (ἀθλητήν), while his house is falling and his children being buried under it; but when his flesh begins to waste away and the hand of the devil is wearing him out with sharper pain than gridirons and furnaces, then the devil brings his wife to him and says, 'How long will you hold out?' She said this, thrusting him into desperation."

The contest is voluntary; and he who enters it needs help from above. St. Matt. XIX, 12: ". . . and there are eunuchs, that made themselves eunuchs for the kingdom of heaven's sake. He that is able to receive it, let him receive it." 58, 600, 33: "This is because that you may learn that the conflict (ἄθλος) is great, not that you should suspect any compulsory allotments. For it is given to those, even to the willing. But He spoke thus to show that much influence from above is needed by him who enters these wrestling-grounds (σκάμμα), whereof he that is willing shall surely partake. For it is customary for Him to use this form of speech, when the good work done is great, as when He says, 'Unto you it is given to know the mysteries [St. Luke VIII, 10].'"

Persevering prayers will bring assistance to our wrestlings. St.

Matt. VII, 7: "Ask, and it shall be given you; seek, and ye shall find; knock, and it shall be opened unto you." 57, 312, 18: "Thus, we are not ourselves, says He, to strive alone, but also to invoke the help from above; and it will surely come and be present with us and will aid us in our struggles (συνεφάψεται τῶν ἀγώνων) and make all easy."

The prayer of the Church is powerful for one who is engaged in wrestling. 54, 587, 9: "Each day let us strip boldly for the contest. In the wordly games, if any one has ten or twenty friends in the crowd, he descends eagerly into the contest (ἀγῶνα). Much more boldly should we do this, having not ten or twenty only, but the entire theatre composed of brothers and fathers. And yet in the worldly contests the spectator is not of much assistance to the contestant, except perchance that he shouts and praises that which is done and, sitting in an upper place, contends with those who speak in a derogatory manner concerning this particular athlete. But to descend into the stadium and grab a hand or pull a foot of the wrestler's opponent or make any other such display, this is not lawful. For those who have been appointed to rule the games plant sharp stakes and place ropes on them and thus restrain the extreme enthusiasm of the spectators. Is it not strange that the spectator is not permitted to descend, when the officials station the trainer beside the dust and command him to give assistance by his knowledge to those who are contending (ἀγωνιζομένοις), but do not allow the spectator to go near? But here it is not so, for both the instructor and the spectator are permitted to descend and standing near us add to our strength by their prayers."

The gifts of God are necessary for our wrestling against unseen powers. 57, 70, 58: "Ask not then of God these things which you receive of the devil. For it is God's part to give a contrite and humbled heart, sober, self-possessed, awestruck, full of repentance and compunction. These are His gifts, forasmuch as it is also of these things that we are most in need. Yea, for a grievous conflict (ἀγών) is at hand, and against the powers unseen is our wrestling (πάλη)."

Salvation came by crucifixion, in which Christ like a wrestler destroyed principalities and powers. St. John III, 14, 15: ". . . even so must the Son of man be lifted up; that whosoever believeth may in him have eternal life." 59, 159, 29: "This is what Paul declares, 'Having despoiled the principalities and the powers, he made a show of them openly, triumphing over them in it [Col. II, 15].' For as some noble champion (ἀθλητής), by lifting on high and dashing down his antagonist, renders his victory more glorious, so Christ, in the sight of all the world, cast down the adverse powers. . . by being hung upon the cross."

It is to crucify Christ a second time to renew those to repentance who fall away. Heb. VI, 4, 6: "For as touching those who . . . then fell away, it is impossible to renew them again unto repentance; seeing they crucify to themselves the Son of God afresh, and put him to an open shame." 63, 79, 22: "It is not possible that Christ should be crucified a second time, for that is to 'put Him to an open shame,' if by death He wrestled with and overcame (κατεπάλαισεν) death."

Christ was desirous of grappling with death itself. 61, 31, 53: "The Jews asked, 'Why did not Christ help Himself on the cross?' He descended not from the cross, not because He could not, but because He would not; for He was hastening on to a close conflict (συμπλακῆναι) with death itself."

Our wrestlings are easier than those of Job because of the coming of Christ. 49, 275, 1: "Job was before the day of grace and of the law, when there was not much strictness of life, when the grace of the Spirit was not so great, when sin was hard to fight against (δυσκαταγώνιστος), when the curse prevailed and when death was terrible. But now our wrestlings (παλαίσματα) have become easier, all these things being removed after the coming of Christ; so that we have no excuse, when we are unable to reach the same standard as He, after so long a time and such advantage and so many gifts given to us by God. Considering therefore all these things, that misfortunes were greater for him and that, when the conflict (ἀγών) was more grievous, then he stripped for the contest (ἀπεδύσατο καὶ ἐπάλαισε), let us bear all that comes upon us nobly and with much thankfulness, in order that we may be able to obtain the same crown as he [Job], by the grace and loving kindness of Jesus Christ our Lord." Since the wrestlings have been made easier because of the coming of Christ, they are also greater: 53, 25, 28; 55, 86, 18; 55, 135, 25; 56, 13, 7.

Christ underwent all things wrestling against the devil, that we might endure greater temptations. 57, 208, 56: "With a view to our instruction He both did and underwent all things; He endured also to be led up thither [into the wilderness] and to wrestle against the devil, in order that each of those who were baptized (if after his baptism he might have to endure greater temptations) might not be troubled as if the result was unexpected, but might continue to endure all nobly, as if happening in the natural course of things."

Our wrestlings have been made easy that we may strive and conquer. 60, 517, 26: "Not even after faith is it possible for a listless man (ῥᾳθυμοῦντα) to be saved! For the wrestlings (παλαί-σματα) are made easy that you may strive (ἀγωνιζόμενος) and conquer, not that you may sleep."

It is our own freedom of will, like that which Job exercised, which determines whether we shall win or not. 64, 521, 49: "There came a day on which the theatre was opened and the athlete descended to the contests (παλαίσματα). But since the holy angels watch over and care for us, the devil works against our salvation. . . . But we conquer or are conquered, not on account of the strength of our opponents or on account of the weakness of the angels who bring help to us, but on account of our own freedom of will."

He who overcomes anger is crowned without the necessity of entering into the wrestling-contest. 60, 348, 41: "If you are insulted and keep silence, then are you strong and the other person weak. You can rejoice because you are crowned and proclaimed conqueror, without having even entered into the contest (ἀγῶνα), without having borne the annoyance of sun and heat and dust, without having grappled (συμπλακείς) with an antagonist and let him close with you (λαβὰς δούς); nothing but a mere wish on your part, sitting or standing, and you have got a mighty crown: a crown far greater than those which the combatants earn; for to throw an opponent (ἀντίπαλον) standing to the encounter is nothing like so great as to overcome the darts of anger."

We need not wrestle at all because of the great power of the Holy Spirit. Eph. VI, 12: "For our wrestling is . . . against the world-rulers of this darkness, against the spiritual hosts of wickedness in the heavenly places." 62, 160, 34: "We wrestle with the darkness by becoming light; so we wrestle against the 'spiritual hosts of wickedness' by becoming good. . . . Our conflict is against spiritual wickedness, because we have an invincible ally, the grace of the Spirit. We have been taught an art, such as shall enable us to wrestle not against men, but against spirits. Nay, if we have a mind, we shall not wrestle at all; for it is because we choose it, that there is a struggle (πάλη), since so great is the power of Him who dwells in us, as He said, 'Behold, I have given you authority to tread upon serpents and scorpions, and over all the power of the enemy [St. Luke X, 19].' All power has He given us, both of wrestling and of not wrestling. It is because we are slothful, that we have to wrestle with them. Paul wrestled not, for he had Satan under his subjection. . . . Hear his words, 'God shall bruise Satan under your feet shortly [Rom. XVI, 20].' . . . . 'I charge thee in the name of Jesus Christ to come out of her [Acts XVI, 18].' And this is not the language of one wrestling; for he who wrestles has not yet conquered, but he who has conquered no longer wrestles."

After having considered all the various phases of this most important contest, it seems natural to close it with some references to those whom St. Chrysostom regarded as notable wrestlers. All are outstanding figures in Holy Writ: Joseph, Abraham, Job, St. Paul and Christ.

Joseph was a skilled wrestler who was able to free himself easily from the holds of Potiphar's wife. 64, 469, 51: "More bitter to him than the abusive language of a mistress was the voice of a flattering woman: 'Lie with me.' The devil stood ready in the adultery as the friend of the groom and shared equally in the attacks made by her. But he did not know that he was wrestling with an athlete skilled in self-control, who freed himself easily from her holds (λαβάς)."

Abraham, like St. Paul, stood nobly in his wrestlings. 61, 388, 8: "Paul's spring of joy was in the comfort of God. Though he grieved as a man, yet he sank not. So too was that patriarch [Abraham] encompassed with joy in the midst of much painful suffering; for consider, he forsook his country, underwent journeyings long and hard; when he came into a strange land, he had 'not so much as to set his foot on [Acts VII, 5].' Then again a famine awaited him which made him once more a wanderer; after the famine came the seizure of his wife, then the fear of death, childlessness, battle, peril, conspiracies, and at the last that crowning contest (ὁ κολοφὼν τῶν ἄθλων): the slaying of his only-begotten and true son. . . . For think not, I pray you, that because he readily obeyed, he felt not all the things which he underwent. . . . But yet none of these things cast him down (κατέβαλεν), but he stood like a noble wrestler (ἀθλητὴς γενναῖος), and for each one was proclaimed (ἀνακηρυττόμενος) and crowned a victor. So also the blessed Paul in his daily trials rejoiced and exulted as though in the mid-delights of paradise."

There are more references to Job as a wrestler than to any other Biblical character. His wrestlings were of the noble and persevering kind which always result in victory. He wrestled in every kind of suffering; and his example is commended to all those who say, "What am I to do? (τί πάθω;)." 61, 389, 10: "Against what martyr then may not Job be worthily set? Surely against ten thousand. For in every kind of suffering he both wrestled (ἐπάλαιε) and was crowned; in goods and children and person and wife and friends and enemies and servants (for these too even spat in his face), in hunger and visions and pains and noisomeness; it was for this I said that he might worthily be set, not against one or two or three, but against ten thousand martyrs."

Job and the Apostles likewise were unmoveable and wrestled and triumphed over all the calamities that befall man. St. Matt. VII, 25: "and the rain descended, and the floods came, and the winds blew, and beat upon that house; and it fell not: for it was founded upon a rock." 57, 323, 45: "By 'rain' here and 'floods' and 'winds' He is expressing metaphorically the calamities and afflictions that befall men, such as false accusations, plots, bereavements, deaths, loss of friends, vexations from strangers, all the ills in our life that any one can mention. . . . Job is our witness, who received all the assaults of the devil and stood unmoveable; and the Apostles, too, are our witnesses, for when the waves of the whole world were beating against them, . . . their soul was not overset (περιέτρεψαν) by them or thrown into despair, but with naked bodies they wrestled, prevailed and triumphed."

Job met all events with a noble and constant spirit. Phil. II, 12: ". . . work out your own salvation with fear and trembling." 62, 243, 49: "When we have persons to cheer and console us in our misfortunes and to hold out to us fair prospects, we yet despond. Consider what it was to have men upbraiding Job. . . . How great an aggravation to find revilers instead of comforters! 'Miserable comforters are ye all [Job XVI, 2],' he says. If we did but revolve these subjects continually in our minds, . . . no ills of this present time could ever have force to disturb our peace, when we turned our eyes to that athlete, that soul of adamant, that spirit impenetrable as brass. For as if he had borne about him a body of brass or stone, he met all events with a noble and constant spirit."

So great was the wrestler Job held in esteem that pilgrimages were made to where his wrestlings took place. 64, 552, 26: "Many to-day undertake long sea-voyages, hastening from the ends of the earth into Arabia, that they may see and kiss the earth which received the contests (σκάμματα) and blood of that crowned athlete, which is more precious than gold."

The fame of Job's wrestling-ground occurs also in 49, 68, 56. "The dung-hill of Job is venerated more than any kingly throne, because from it one may derive all manner of help and exhortation in the cause of endurance. Therefore to this day many undertake a long pilgrimage as far as Arabia, that they may see that dung-hill and, having beheld it, may kiss the earth which contained the wrestling-ground (σκάμματα) of such a victor (στεφανίτου) and received the blood that was more precious than all gold! For the purple shines not so brilliantly, as did that body when dyed not in another's blood, but in its own! . . . . Figure to yourselves then this wrestler (ἀθλητήν); and imagine that you see that dung-hill and Job himself sitting in the midst of it!"

Whoever imitates the athlete Job will be able to contend nobly against the devil. 64, 656, 29: "Whoever reads this book [Job], beholding this noble athlete as an original image, let him imitate his courage, have zeal for his endurance, in order that he may contend nobly against all the wiles of the devil and be able to obtain the good things promised to those who love God."

St. Paul is the outstanding wrestler of the New Testament, as Job is of the Old. To this athlete is attributed the reason for the Christians first being called such in Antioch. Acts XI, 25, 26: "And he [Barnabas] went forth to Tarsus to seek for Saul; and when he had found him, he brought him unto Antioch." 60, 192, 30: "He came to the athletic wrestler (ἀθλητήν). . . . Verily this is the reason why it was there that they were appointed to be called Christians, because Paul there spent so long a time!"

The Christian should live in such a way that he may be counted worthy of beholding this wrestler. 60, 678, 20: "May we not only hear Paul's voice here, but hereafter, when we are departed, may we also be counted worthy to see this wrestler (ἀθλητήν) of Christ."

Christ is represented as being the supreme wrestler and an example to all. This is based on the interpretation of Heb. II, 10: "For it became him [God], for whom are all things, and through whom are all things, in bringing many sons unto glory, to make the author of their salvation perfect through sufferings." 63, 40, 15: "And what he says is this: 'He has done what is worthy of His love toward mankind, in showing His first-born to be more glorious than all and in setting Him forth as an example to the others, like some noble wrestler (ἀθλητὴν γενναῖον) who surpasses the rest.'"

4. BOXING[1]

Boxing was the most formidable of all the contests. Evidences as to the fearfulness of this bloody spectacle will be noticed throughout the chapter. This contest was accordingly entered with fear and trembling. We are apprised of this fact, when St. Chrysostom in speaking against luxury tells how the one who has prepared a banquet fears the envy of accusers. 62, 306, 35: "One may see the man who has prepared a sumptuous table in greater fear than those who are going to fight a boxing-match (πυκτεύειν), lest aught should turn out other than was expected, lest he should be shot with the glance of envy, and thereby should procure himself a multitude of accusers."

The boxing-contest brings the boxer into action and enables him to shine more than when he is in training. This is drawn from the comment on II Cor. I, 6: "But whether we are afflicted, it is for your comfort and salvation . . . which worketh in the patient enduring of the same sufferings which we also suffer." 61, 392, 34: "For as a pugilist (παγκρατιαστής) is an object of admiration, when he but shows himself and is in good training and has his skill within himself,

---

[1]No other sport was older and none other was more popular at all times among the Greeks than boxing. The history of Greek boxing may be divided into three main periods. The first is the period of the soft thongs which were made of ox-hide, raw or simply dressed with oil or fat so as to render them supple; this period extends from Homeric times to the close of the sixth century. The second is that of the sharp thongs and *sphairai*, or gloves, formed from thick bands of some soft substance, leaving the fingers free, but extending almost the whole length of the forearm, bound round by stout and stiff leather thongs fastened apparently between the fingers and the thumb. These gloves continued in use with but little variation till at least the second century A. D. Indeed it is doubtful if any other form was ever used in the true Greek festivals. The third period is that of the weighted *caestus*, which is a purely Roman invention, utterly barbarous and entirely fatal to all science in boxing. The Roman *caestus* may have been used in some of those gladitorial shows which found favor in certain parts of Greece under the Empire, but it was never used at Olympia, or indeed at any place where any vestige of the athletic tradition of Greece yet lingered. There were no rounds in Greek boxing: the opponents fought to a finish. It might happen that both were too exhausted and by mutual consent paused to take breath; but usually the fight went on until one of the two either was incapable of fighting any more or acknowledged himself defeated by holding up his hand. Classification by weights was unknown to the Greeks. Their competitions were open to all comers whatever their weight, and weight had perhaps even greater advantage than it has to-day. The Greek boxer confined his attention almost exclusively to his opponent's head. Whether it was that he did not realize the use of body-blows or that he considered them "bad form" or that they were prohibited, it is certain that he made little or no use of them.

but when he is in action (ἐνεργῇ), enduring blows and striking his adversary, then most of all shines forth, because then his good training (εὐεξία) is most put into action (ἐνεργεῖται) and the proof of his skill evidently shown, thus your salvation is more especially put into action, that is, is displayed, increased, heightened, when it has endurance, when it suffers and bears all things nobly."

Job was struck with a malignant ulcer in order that his virtue might shine forth the more. 64, 549, 42: "His whole body was made one sore (τραῦμα, 'wound') in order that the virtue of the crowned athlete (στεφανίτης) might shine forth from all members."

St. Chrysostom heartens Stagirius in discouragement (47, 446, 36) by explaining that the devil makes us more magnificent by reason of our encounters with him. "Now when you have thrown everything away and vowed yourself to God and this demon jumps out at you, you express surprise as to why none of the spectators is disturbed; but he who is enrolled in the number of the boxers and, being trained (γυμνασθέντι), goes into the contest (ἀγῶνα), the combatant (ἀνταγωνιστής) seeks this one of all, striking (πατάσσων) his head and hitting (κόπτων) his face. Now this is not strange nor should it be a cause for discouragement, if that boxer [the devil] should vex and torment us; for this is the law of those who box (πυκτευόντων). But if he turns us round and knocks us down (περιτρέπει καὶ καταβάλλει) and goes off with the prize (βραβεῖον), this is a shame. But as long as he does not prevail and not only injures us not, but also renders us the greatest benefit, he makes us more magnificent by that strenuous encounter (τῇ σφοδρᾷ συμπλοκῇ)."

The next point, after considering the reasons for the boxing-contest, is that the contest is here and now. 62, 645, 54: "It is impossible for a man who is fighting with evil not to be exposed to tribulation. One cannot be in a boxing-combat and live luxuriously; one cannot be wrestling and feasting. Let none therefore of those who are contending (ἀθλούντων) seek for ease or joyous living. The present state is a contest (ἀγών) and the very scene of conflicts (ἀγώνων τὸ στάδιον). The season for rest is not now; this is the time for toil and labor. No one who has just stripped and anointed himself thinks of ease. If you think of ease, why did you strip or prepare to box (χεῖρας ἀντῆρας)? 'But do I not maintain the fight (ἀνταίρω)?' you say. What, when you do not conquer your desires or resist the evil bias of nature?"

In discussing the persecution of St. Stephen (60, 123, 54) the idea is again presented that the present life is a contest. "The present affliction is the cause of rest. 'This sickness,' says He, 'is not unto death [St. John XI, 4].' The present life is a contest (ἀγών); if so, it is our business to fight (ι υκτεύειν) now."

In 63, 51, 40 the present is the season for contending and bearing blows as does the boxer. "Let us not seek relaxation. ... No noble-spirited athlete (γενναῖος ἀθλητής), when in the lists (σκάμματι), seeks for baths and a table full of food and wine. This is not for an athlete, but for a sluggard. For the athlete contends with dust, with oil, with the heat of the sun's rays, with much sweat, with pressure and constraint. This is the time for contest and for boxing (πυκτεύ-ειν); therefore also for being wounded and bloody and in pain. Hear what the blessed Paul says, 'So fight I, as not beating the air [I Cor. IX, 26].' Let us consider that our whole life is in combats (βίον ἐναγώνιον), and then we shall never seek rest, we shall never feel it strange when we are afflicted: no more than a boxer (πύκτης) feels it strange, when he is in the contest (ἐν ἀγῶνι). There is another season for repose."

The reflection on the conflict of Job (64, 545, 4) presents the idea of never taking time to pause in the boxing-match. "Therefore while we are on earth let us not pause (ἀναπνεύσωμεν), but always engage in the boxing-match (πυκτεύωμεν), especially in the time of sickness, when pains are everywhere disturbing the soul, when the devil is standing by us, urging us to speak some bitter word."

The boxer does not concern himself about ornament, but only how he may win. In expounding I Tim. II, 9: ". . . that women adorn themselves in modest apparel . . ." St. Chrysostom declares (62, 543, 13): "You have taken upon you a great contest (ἀγῶνα), where combat (ἀθλήσεως), not ornament is required; where the boxing-contest (πυκτεύειν) awaits you, not sloth and ease. Do you not observe those who box and contend in the games? Do they concern themselves about their walk or their dress? Nay; but scorning all these and throwing about them a garment dripping with oil (ἱμάτιον ἐλαίῳ διάβροχον), they look only to one thing, to wound (πλῆξαι) and not to be wounded."

Those should be admired who know how to endure calamities, just as we applaud those in the games who are not vexed by the blows which they receive. 61, 256, 17: "In men's calamities it is not those who suffer great evils whom we lament and account wretched, but those who know not how to bear them, even though they are small. Whereas he who knows how to bear them is, as all know, worthy of praises and crowns. And to prove that this is so, whom do we applaud in the games (ἀγῶσι)? Those who are much beaten and do not vex themselves, but hold their heads on high, or those who fly after the first strokes? Are not those even crowned by us as manly and noble, while we laugh at these as unmanly and cowards? So then let us do in the affairs of life. Him who bears all easily let us crown, as we do that noble champion (γενναῖον παγκρατιαστήν); but weep over him who shrinks and trembles at his dangers and who, before he receives the blow, is dead with fear. For so in the games; if any one before he raised his hands, at the mere sight of his adversary extending his right hand, should fly, though receiving no blow, he will be laughed to scorn as feeble and effeminate and unversed in such struggles. Now this is what happens to those who fear poverty and cannot so much as endure the expectation of it."

The same reason for patiently enduring the contest occurs in the exposition of I Tim. VI, 12: "Fight the good fight of the faith (ἀγωνίζου τὸν καλὸν ἀγῶνα τῆς πίστεως), lay hold on the life eternal . . . ." 62, 594, 9: "There is need not only of profession, but of patience also to persevere in that profession and of vehement contention (ἀγῶνος σφοδροῦ) and of numberless toils, that you may not be overthrown (περιτραπῆναι). . . . As in the games, he who does not earnestly covet the crown may from the first surrender himself to revellings and drunkenness; and so in fact do the cowardly and unmanly combatants (πυκτευόντων), while those who look steadfastly to the crown sustain blows without number (μυρίας πληγάς), for they are supported and roused to action by the hope of future reward."

David is a splendid example of one who rose again after having received a most terrific blow, an achievement of which his son, Solomon, was incapable. 61, 562, 21: "The desire for beauty overcame even the great prophet David. . . . After him it took possession of his son still more completely. And yet there was never man wiser than he, and all other virtue did he attain; still, however, he was seized so violently by this passion, that even in his vitals he received the wound (πληγήν). And the father indeed rose (ἀνέστη) again and renewed the struggle and was crowned again; but the son showed nothing of the kind."

St. Paul in his boxing and running increased his earnestness as he neared the prize. 61, 574, 32: "He entered into the world as if into a race-course (στάδιον) and, having stripped himself before all, he so made a noble stand (ἵστατο γενναίως). For he knew the fiends that were boxing (πυκτεύοντας) with him. Wherefore also he shone forth brightly at once from the beginning, from the very starting-post (βαλβῖδος), and even to the end he continued the same, yea, rather he even increased his earnestness (διωγμόν) as he drew nearer the prize (βραβείου)."

The persecution of St. Paul at Lystra leads St. Chrysostom to remark on the smarts inflicted by words as well as by stones, and how the boxer bears his smarts kindly. 60, 231, 28: "If one insults you, hold your peace and bless if you can,—and you have given a lesson of gentleness and meekness. I know that many do not so smart under wounds, as they do under the blow which is inflicted by words. But let us not smart or, rather feeling the smart, let us endure. Do you not see the pugilists (πυκτεύοντας), how with their heads sorely battered they bite their teeth into their lips and so bear their smarts kindly? . . . Remember Paul: reflect that you, the beaten, have conquered and that he, the beater, is defeated."

Job in his poverty is also a shining example of the victorious boxer. 64, 553, 23: "You see how much poverty is preferred to wealth and sickness to health, and how temptation is better than rest for those who are sober, and how it makes those who struggle (ἀθλοῦντας) more brilliant and more energetic. Who has seen, who has heard of so marvellous struggles? The boxers (πύκται) in the games, when they knock off (κατακόψωσι) the heads of their opponents, then conquer and are crowned. But the devil, when he had battered (κατέκοψε) the body of the righteous man with sores everywhere and had made him weaker, was then conquered and retreated."

The practised pugilist unnerves the strength of his opponent by not returning blows; so one who is injuriously treated completely unnerves the other person, if he makes no return. 60, 118, 56: "The striker, if he has to do with one who yields, is the sooner unnerved, and his blow is spent upon himself. For no practised pugilist (ἄνθρωπος παγκρατιάζειν εἰδώς) so unnerves the strength of his antagonist, as does a man who being injuriously treated makes no return. For the other only goes off ashamed and condemned, first by his own conscience and secondly by all the spectators."

A similar idea is conveyed in the comment on Rom. XII, 21: "Be not overcome of evil, but overcome evil with good." 60, 612, 38: "This is a victory; for the boxer (πυκτεύων) is rather then the conqueror, not when he brings himself under to take the blows, but when he withdraws himself and makes his antagonist waste his strength upon the air (εἰς τὸν ἀέρα κενοῦν τὴν δύναμιν). And in this way he will not be struck himself and will also exhaust the whole of the other's strength."

The exegesis of St. Matt. V, 27, 28 admonishes us that, if we open our mind to the devil, it will be harder to repulse him. "Ye have heard that it was said, Thou shalt not commit adultery: but I say unto you, that every one that looketh on a woman to lust after her hath committed adultery with her already in his heart." 57, 256, 55: "For in truth greater is the struggle (ἀγών) on beholding and not possessing the object of fondness; nor is the pleasure so great which we reap from the sight as the mischief which we undergo from increasing this desire, thus making our opponent (ἀνταγωνιστήν) strong and giving more scope (εὐρυχωρίαν) to the devil and no longer being able to repulse (ἀποκρούσασθαι) him, now that we have brought him into our inmost parts and have thrown our mind open to him. Therefore He says, 'Commit not adultery with your eyes, and you will commit none with your mind.'"

Abraham is pictured as a glorious boxer standing before all blows. 61, 388, 13: "He forsook his country, underwent journeyings long and hard; when he came into a strange land, he had 'not so much as to set his foot on [Acts VII, 5].' Then again a famine awaited him which made him once more a wanderer; after the famine came the seizure of his wife, then the fear of death, childlessness, battle, peril, conspiracies, and at the last that crowning contest (ὁ κολοφὼν τῶν ἄθλων): the slaying of his only-begotten and true son, that grievous and irreparable [sacrifice]. . . . For though his righteousness had been, as indeed it was, inestimable, yet was he a man and felt as nature bade. But yet none of these things cast him down, but he stood like a noble athlete, and for each one was proclaimed and crowned a victor."

A few instances occur of the use of the term καιρία πληγή, which in boxing-parlance may be called a "knockout-blow."

Joseph delivers a "knockout-blow" to Potiphar's wife in 54, 538, 4. "In order that Joseph might give her the deadly blow (καιρίαν πληγήν) and remind her of the goodness of her lord and persuade her not to be so ungrateful to him, Joseph says, 'Thou art outside my power, because thou art his wife; how then can I do this great wickedness, and sin against God [Gen. XXXIX, 9]?' . . . He stood his ground in this contest (ἀγῶνα) not once or twice, but many times as the Scripture says, 'As she spake to Joseph day by day, he hearkened not unto her [ib. v. 10].'"

St. Paul strikes home the blow in the case of the Jews, who had not attained even to the righteousness which was by the law. Rom. IX, 30, 31: "What shall we say then? That the Gentiles, who followed not after righteousness, attained to righteousness, even the righteousness which is of faith: but Israel, following after a law of righteousness, did not arrive at that law." 60, 563, 20: "Paul seems to be indulging them by saying, 'following after.' But afterward he strikes the blow home (καιρίαν ἐπάγει τὴν πληγήν). He shows that before the faith even on their own ground they were worsted and condemned. 'For you, O Jew,' he says, 'have not found even the righteousness which was by the law.'"

Satan in his temptation of Christ was given deadly blows. 57, 212, 21: "Marvel not, if Satan in reasoning with Christ often turns himself about (περιτρέπεται). For as pugilists (πυκτεύοντες), when they have received deadly blows (καιρίας πληγάς), reel about drenched in much blood and blinded, even so Satan, too, darkened by the first and the second blow, speaks at random what comes uppermost and proceeds to his third assault."

The devil in the person of death received a "knockout-blow" from Christ on the cross. The comment is on Col. II, 15: "having despoiled the principalities and the powers, he made a show of them openly, triumphing over them in it." 62, 341, 12: "The devil [i. e., death] received his fatal blow (καιρίαν πληγήν) from a dead body on the cross. And as an athlete, when he thinks he has hit his adversary (ἀντίπαλον), himself receives a fatal blow (καιρίαν πληγήν), so truly does Christ also show that to die with confidence is the devil's shame."

After considering some notable victories, we pass now to the refreshment of the boxer. Almsgiving is most efficient to the Christian combatant in his struggles, such as covetousness, anger and pride. 59, 442, 13: "Almsgiving enlightens the soul, making it sleek (λιπαίνει), beautiful and vigorous. Not so does the fruit of the olive uphold the athletes, as this oil refreshes (ἀνακτᾶται) the combatants (ἀγωνιστάς) of piety. Let us then anoint our hands, that we may raise them well against our adversary (ἀντίπαλον)."

St. Paul comes to the people of Rome for refreshment. Rom. XV, 32: "that I may come unto you in joy through the will of God, and together with you find rest." 60, 663, 33: "He has been engaged in strife and conflict (ἀγωνιζόμενος καὶ πυκτεύων) and comes to be refreshed with them. This is to gratify them and to make them more cheerful by sharing with them his crown and to show that they too struggle (ἀγωνιζομένους) and labor."

St. Paul gives encouragement to boxers in Heb. XII, 12: "Wherefore lift up the hands that hang down, and the palsied knees." 63, 209, 47: "He speaks as to boxers (πύκτας). Do you see how he encourages (ἐπαίρει) them?"

The last point for consideration in this chapter is that of shadow-boxing (σκιαμαχία), a vain and futile contest in which the Christian

Boxer is secure from injuries at the hands of his adversary. St. Chrysostom in addressing the people of Antioch (49, 74, 18) shows them how he who lives virtuously cannot be injured. "As he, who boxes with a shadow and beats the air (ἀέρα δέρων), will be unable to hit any one, so he, who is at war with the just man, is but striking at a shadow (σκιαμαχεῖ) and wasting his own strength, without being able to inflict any injury upon him. Grant me then to be sure of the kingdom of heaven; and, if you wish, slay me this day."

St. Paul was not only an eminent runner and wrestler, but a famous boxer as well; so it is fitting to close this section with the metaphor which is based on Col. IV, 3: ". . . to speak the mystery of Christ, for which I am also in bonds." 62, 371, 7: "A prisoner is in fear, when there is nothing beyond bonds; but one who despises death, how shall he be bound? They did the same as if they had put in bonds the shadow of Paul and had gagged its mouth. For it was a fighting with a shadow (σκιομαχία);[1] for he was both more tenderly regretted by his friends and more reverenced by his enemies, as bearing the prize (ἔπαθλον) for courage in his bonds."

---

[1]St. Chrysostom here uses the later spelling of σκιαμαχία.

5. CHARIOT-RACING[1]

The people whom St. Chrysostom addressed had a particular fondness for the chariot-race, and its fascination was almost irresistible to them. The charioteers were greatly admired for their skill and dexterity, and their partisans lavished all manner of praise upon them. However, their social station must have been quite low; and, certainly, runners, wrestlers and boxers must have ranked higher in this respect, as we do not find any such derogatory statements made about them as about charioteers. We may infer the social status of the charioteer from St. Chrysostom's arraignment of the people (59, 320, 44), who know all about the art of a charioteer but not about that of being a Christian. "If a man calls you a charioteer, you say that you have been insulted and use every means to wipe off the affront; but if he draws you to be a spectator of the action, you do not start away and the art, whose name you shun, you almost in every case pursue. But where you ought to have both the action and the name, both to be and to be called a Christian, you do not even know what kind of thing the action is."

The charioteer's status is still further indicated in 60, 213, 10. "There are no right judgments in the populace; they that minister to their lusts, those are the persons whom they admire. And if you would see proof of this, mark those who give away their substance to the harlots, to the charioteers ($\dot{\eta}\nu\iota\dot{o}\chi\iota\varsigma$), to the dancers."

The charioteer was highly championed by his adherents. This is learned from the following statement, 59, 112, 19. "The heathen,

---

[1]The oldest and most aristocratic of all the events at the funeral games of Patroclus described in the *Iliad* is the chariot-race (in which the war-chariot is used), the monopoly of the nobles then, as it was always later the sport of kings and the rich. The usual course was two stades long. The circuit of the course at Olympia was eight stades, or nearly a mile; however, the actual course traversed by the horses measured from pillar to pillar and back was only six stades. Positions were assigned by lot; and undoubtedly the chariots on the left had a slight advantage in point of distance. It appears that a rope was stretched in front of the whole line, which was dropped or removed at the moment of starting. The signal for the start was given by a trumpet. The fully developed programme comprised six events: three for full-grown horses, three for colts, for each class a four-horse-chariot-race, a horse-race, and a pair-horse-chariot-race. The four-horse-chariots ran twelve times round the course, the pair-horse-chariots eight times, the colts' pair-horse-chariot-race three times. At some point, perhaps at the turn of the last lap, a trumpet was blown. Chariot-racing was a costly amusement and in the century before our era it disappeared from the programme of Olympia, doubtless because of want of competitors. It was restored spasmodically under the Empire, but never recovered its old position in Greece.

although established in a lie, use every means to conceal the shamefulness of their opinions, while we, the servants of truth, cannot even open our mouths. . . . They who admire a charioteer use every exertion and contrivance not to come off worst in any dispute concerning him and they string together long panegyrics, as they compose their defense against those who find fault with them and cast sneers without number at their opponents."

The knowledge of people about charioteers and horses was far in advance of that about Scripture. 59, 321, 4: "There are some who, if you ask who was Amos or Obadiah or what is the number of the Prophets or Apostles, cannot even open their mouth; but for horses and charioteers they compose excuses [arguments for defense] more cleverly than sophists or rhetoricians; and after all this they say, 'What is the harm? What is the loss?'"

Practically the same sentiment is expressed in 59, 187, 37. "Is it not strange that those who sit by the market can tell the names and families and cities of charioteers and the kinds of power possessed by each and can give exact account of the good or bad qualities of the very horses, but that those who come hither should know nothing of what is done here, but should be ignorant of the number even of the Sacred Books?"

In the spiritual chariot-race the first requisite is that of having a charioteer over the conscience. St. Chrysostom, after stating that in spiritual matters we must have laborious beginnings as we do in the education of our children, says (61, 118, 31): "We must set a charioteer over our conscience, who will not allow us to indulge our appetite (γαστρίζεσθαι), but make us run and strive mightily (τρέχειν καὶ ἀγωνίζεσθαι)."

That God should be the charioteer over our life is based on the interpretation of Rom. VIII, 14: "For as many as are led by the the Spirit of God, these are the sons of God." 60, 525, 35: "Paul wishes to show that God should use such power over our life—not only the body, but the soul also, as a charioteer over a pair of horses."

One who succumbs to passion is virtually flinging the charioteer from his own horses. 60, 126, 41: "It is not possible to be master of one's self when in a passion. . . . If you succumb to passion, you have flung your own charioteer from his horses, you have got him dragging along the ground upon his back. And it is all one, as if one driver (ἡνίοχος), being in a passion with another, should choose to be dragged along thus."

Discoursing on the subject of being temperate, the point is made that no harm is suffered, if reason as the charioteer keeps the horses

under control. 61, 144, 63: "For over us is a charioteer, even reason:
and the reins are the body, connecting the horses with the charioteer;
if then these are in good condition, you will suffer no harm; but if
you let them go, you have annihilated and ruined everything. . . .
Set the charioteer upon the car and bend the eye of your mind toward
God. For in all other cases he that appoints the games contributes
nothing, but only awaits the end. But in this case, he is all in all,
who appointed the contest ($\dot{\alpha}\gamma\omega\nu o\theta\acute{\epsilon}\tau\eta s$), even God."

The necessity for reason keeping its proper place on the chariot
relates to I Cor. XIV, 40: ". . . let all things be done decently and in
order." 61, 318, 28: "This may be observed in other than spiritual
matters. . . . As in a chariot if you confound the order and cast the
greater out of its proper place and bring the lesser into its rank, you
destroy all, and things are turned upside down. Let us therefore
not destroy our order by casting down right reason and setting our
lusts, passions and pleasure over the rational part."[1]

That the flesh must not get the mastery of the Christian Charioteer is founded on the exegesis of Eph. II, 16: "and might reconcile
them both [carnal and spiritual desires] in one body unto God through
the cross. . . ." 62, 41, 22: "Nothing that is natural is evil. Why
then does he call carnal affections sins?—because whenever the
flesh exalts itself and gets the mastery over its charioteer, it pro-
duces ten thousand mischiefs. The virtue of the flesh is its subjection to the soul. It is its vice to govern the soul. As the horse
then may be good and nimble (and yet this is not shown without a
rider), so also the flesh will then show its goodness, when we cut off
its prancings ($\sigma\kappa\iota\rho\tau\acute{\eta}\mu\alpha\tau\alpha$). . . . The rider to be properly skilful
must have the Spirit at hand to impart new strength to the rider."

That the mind as charioteer must be put over anger and desire is
drawn from Eph. V, 4: ". . . nor foolish talking, or jesting, which are
not befitting. . . ." 62, 120, 52: "When we shall have disciplined
these two faculties of the soul, anger and desire, and have put them
like well-broken horses under the yoke of reason, then let us set
over them the mind as charioteer, that we may 'gain the prize
($\beta\rho\alpha\beta\epsilon\hat{\iota}o\nu$) of our high calling [Phil. III, 14].'"

The successful charioteer heeds not the plaudits of the multitude,
but regards only the king who is present in the rôle of judge. 63,
675, 34: "In the horse-races ($\iota\pi\pi o\delta\rho o\mu\acute{\iota}\alpha\iota s$) those who are driving the
horses, when all the people are applauding and pouring forth number-

---

[1]The same comment is also made (53, 189, 45) in reference to Gen. VI, 2:
". . . the sons of God saw the daughters of men that they were fair; and they took
them wives of all that they chose."

less favorable acclamations (μυρίας εὐφημίας), are not turned or reap any pleasure from their acclamations, but look to one alone, the king who is sitting in the midst, and pay attention to his nod and overlook (ὑπερορῶσι, 'scorn') the whole multitude and then take great glory when he honors them by crowning [them]. Therefore what would be more wretched for those who show their skill for display to men?.... What do you, O man? Are you going to call another as witness of those things which you do? Do you not have another judge and another spectator? Do you not see the charioteers who, when all the city is sitting above, in the horse-races running about the whole course of the stadium, then strive to overthrow the chariots of their opponents, when they see the king sitting? Of so many eyes they consider only one as being more trustworthy. But seeing the King of angels Himself as judge (ἀγωνοθετοῦντα) at your race (δρόμοις), do you abandon Him for the sight of those who are like yourself? And it is for this very reason that after numberless contests, after much sweating you depart without the crown and go away without the reward (βραβείων) into the presence of the judge (ἀγωνοθέτην).'' The same idea of charioteers disregarding the multitude and looking only to the king is also found in 53, 54, 11 and 56, 113, 51, the latter instance being used of King Uzziah, who did that which was right in the sight of the Lord.

In the Christian chariot-race humility shows its superiority over pride. 51, 311, 1: "When lately we mentioned the Pharisee and the publican and when we hypothetically yoked two chariots from virtue and vice, we indicated each truth, how great is the humbleness of mind and how great the danger of pride. For this, even when conjoined with righteousness and fastings and tithes, fell behind (ὑστέρησεν), while that, even when yoked with sin, outstripped (προέλαβε) the Pharisee's pair, even though its charioteer was a poor one."

A little later (ib. 312, 12), while still discoursing on the progress of the Gospel, the same metaphor is more highly elaborated. "Now if the confidence which they who confess their own sins effect for themselves is so great, how great crowns will they not win, who are conscious of many good qualities, yet humble their own souls? For when sinfulness is yoked with humbleness of mind, it runs with such ease as to pass and outstrip (ὑπερβῆναι καὶ προλαβεῖν) righteousness combined with pride. If therefore you have yoked it with righteousness, whither will it not reach? Through how many heavens will it not pass? By the throne of God it will stay its course, in the midst of the angels, with much confidence."

This chapter also will be brought to an end by a reference to St.

Paul, although rather indirectly in this instance. Commenting on Phil. II, 5–8: "Have this mind in you, which was also in Christ Jesus. . . and being found in fashion as a man, he humbled himself, becoming obedient even unto death, yea, the death of the cross," St. Chrysostom exhorts his congregation to rouse themselves against all heresies, stating the great pleasure derived from overthrowing them in the manner of a charioteer. 62, 219, 4: "For if, when chariots contend in the horse-race (ἐν ταῖς τῶν ἵππων ἀμίλλαις), there is nothing so pleasing as when one of them dashes against and over-throws whole chariots with their drivers and, after throwing down many with the charioteers who stood thereon, drives by alone toward the goal (νύσσαν) and the end of the course and, amid the applause and clamor which rise on all sides to heaven, with coursers winged as it were by that joy and that applause, sweeps over the whole ground (τὸ στάδιον ἅπαν διατρέχῃ), how much greater will the pleasure be here, when by the grace of God we overthrow at once and in a body the combinations and devilish machinations of all these heresies together with their charioteers?"

6. THE CONTEST IN GENERAL

After having treated the four major contests in the games, there still remains a number of references which bear upon the Christian Contest in a general way and which do not admit of specific application to running, wrestling, boxing and chariot-racing. These will accordingly be classified by themselves in the present chapter, which will have much the same order of arrangement as the preceding chapters. It will be noted that many of the notions in this chapter are not entirely new. However, their presentation here may serve as a recapitulation of much that has been written in the earlier chapters, as well as an introduction of new ideas in their proper place.

Brilliant as the crown was, yet a contest, such as Abraham endured when on the point of sacrificing Isaac, might outshine numberless crowns. 61, 414, 24: "This contest (ἆθλος) outshines innumerable crowns (στεφάνων ἀπείρων)."

The comment on St. Matt. V, 13: "Ye are the salt of the earth . . ." indicates that the Christian's contest is not an ordinary one. "Think not then," He says, "that you are drawn into ordinary conflicts (τοὺς τυχόντας ἀγῶνας) or that for some small matters you are to give account (57, 231, 29)."

That the Christian contest should naturally be greater is derived from the text of St. Matt. V, 20: "For I say unto you, that except your righteousness shall exceed the righteousness of the scribes and Pharisees, ye shall in no wise enter into the kingdom of heaven." 57, 244, 14: "Observe the increase of grace: in that He will have His newly-come disciples better than the teachers in the Old Covenant. . . . The old law does not now bring into the kingdom those who live after the coming of Christ, favored as they are with more strength and bound to strive (ἀγωνίζεσθαι) for greater things."

In the Christian contest there is required only what is reasonable, therefore there is no excuse for any one living in wickedness. 61, 21, 10: "You, perhaps, though living with a wife, are not chaste; but another even without a wife keeps his chastity inviolate. Now what excuse have you for not keeping the rule, while another even leaps beyond the bounds (σκάμματα πηδῶντος) that have been drawn to mark it?"

The same idea is somewhat more elaborated in 57, 438, 28. "What plea will you have, when others are leaping beyond the bounds (σκάμματα πηδώντων) and you yourself too slothful for what is enacted [i. e., the injunctions of Christ]? Thus you we admonish to give alms of such things as you have, but another has even stripped himself of all his possessions; you we require to live chastely with your wife, but another has not so much as entered into marriage; and you we entreat not to be envious, but another we find giving up even his own life for charity; you again we entreat to be lenient in judgments and not severe to those who sin, but another, even when smitten, has turned the other cheek also. . . . Let us then bear in mind these things and not be torpid in our career (δρόμους) for virtue's sake; but having stripped ourselves with all readiness for these glorious wrestlings (παλαίσματα), let us labor for a little while, that we may win the perpetual and imperishable crowns (διηνεκεῖς καὶ ἀμαράντους στεφάνους)." The same sentiment on torpidity in the contests of virtue occurs in 53, 321, 48.

The reasonableness of the contest is still further indicated in 62, 194, 30. "Let us not be sluggish. God has placed before us contests within measure (συμμέτρους ἀγῶνας), having no toil. Yet let us not despise them for this. . . . Are you unable to live a virgin life. You are permitted to marry. Are you unable to strip yourself of all which you have? You are permitted to supply the needs of others from what you have, 'your abundance being a supply for their want [II Cor. VIII, 14].'"

In training the disciples (St. Matt. X, 28: "And be not afraid of them that kill the body, but are not able to kill the soul. . . ."), Christ signifies that the contests are not hard (57, 401, 22): "For even should they prevail, it will be over the inferior part, I mean, the body. . . . See you how he signifies that the conflicts are to be easy (ἀγῶνας εὐχερεῖς)?—because, in truth, death did exceedingly agitate their souls, inspiring terror for a time, for it [death] had not as yet been made easy to overcome (εὐκαταγώνιστος), nor had they who were to despise it partaken of the grace of the Spirit."

Allowance is made for the difficulty of the contest. This is adduced from the exegesis of the parable of the Ten Virgins (St. Matt. XXV, 1–13). 58, 711, 41: "Christ puts forth this parable sufficient to persuade them that virginity, though it should have everything else, if destitute of the good things arising out of almsgiving, is ejected with the harlots. And most reasonably; for the one was overcome by the love of carnal pleasure, but these of money. But the love of carnal pleasure and that of money are not equal, but that of carnal pleasure is far keener and more tyrannical. And the weaker the antagonist (ἀνταγωνιστής), the less excusable are these who are overcome (νικηθεῖσαι) thereby. Therefore also He calls them foolish, for, having undergone the greater labor, they have betrayed all for want of the less."

It is suggested that the Christian Athlete should be grateful for his contests, such as St. Paul enumerates in II Cor. XI, 27: ". . . in hunger and thirst, in fastings often, in cold and nakedness." 61, 571, 38: "Paul had not even a full supply of necessary food, or even of thin clothing, but the champion (ἀγωνιστής) of the world wrestled in nakedness and boxed with hunger,—so far was he from enriching himself. Yet he murmured not, but was grateful for these things to the Judge of the contest (ἀγωνοθέτη)."

The cheerfulness of Abraham in undergoing his contests is shown in the comment on Gen. XV, 1: ". . . Fear not, Abram: I am thy shield, and thy exceeding great reward." 53, 333, 5: "This just man is able to teach all of us to strip eagerly for the contests (ἀγῶνας) of virtue, being confident of the rewards above, and to receive cheerfully all those things which are considered hard for the present life, being supported by the hope of the rewards." The same promise stirs the athlete of piety and nerves his soul (ib. 338, 8), while the promise of Gen. XII, 7: ". . . Unto thy seed will I give this land . . . ." makes the athlete active and youthful for the contests of famine and barrenness in Canaan (ib. 334, 21).

St. Paul shows the love of God toward the struggler in Rom. VIII, 21: ". . . the creation itself also shall be delivered from the bondage of corruption. . . ." 60, 530, 59: "Man takes the lead in all respects, and it is for his sake that all things are made. See how Paul solaces the struggler (ἀγωνιζόμενον) and shows the unspeakable love of God toward man."

Likewise in speaking of the afflictions which Abraham had to undergo (53, 304, 38), St. Chrysostom shows that they are really a sign of divine providence and should be regarded as contests (ἀγῶνες), that we might be held more worthy of honor.

The folly of one who postpones baptism till his last gasp is given in 60, 24, 21. "For indeed both by works and by words must we show our good will toward Him. Now what you are doing is all one, as if an athlete should want to strip for the contest, just when the spectators have risen from their seats."

Those who are once in the contest do not become frightened. St. Peter and St. John bear witness of this by their intrepid behavior, when threatened by the chief priests. 60, 87, 24: "See the difficulty in which they are and how the fear of men again does everything. As in the case of Christ, for all their hindrance, the faith did but gain ground the more; so was it now. . . . O the folly to suppose that those who had tasted of the conflict (ἀγώνων) would now take fright at it! . . . Behold the greatness of mind in the Apostles! 'But Peter and John answered and said unto them, Whether it is right in the sight of God to hearken unto you rather than unto God, judge ye [Acts IV, 19].'"

Christ is the supreme example of agony before the crucifixion, but on the cross He did everything without being troubled. 59, 461, 53: "Do you consider, I pray, how even on the cross He did everything without being troubled, speaking with the disciple concerning His mother, fulfilling prophecies, holding forth good hopes to the thief. Yet before He was crucified, He appeared sweating, agonized, fearing. . . . By these two things He teaches us, even if before things terrible we are troubled, not on that account to shrink from things terrible, but, when we have entered into the contest (ἀγῶνα), to deem all things possible and easy. Let us not then tremble at death, if we are dragged to it for the sake of what is pleasing to God, but boldly strip for it, preferring the future to the present life."

One who flees from a contest is never honored. In commenting on the psalm which David composed when he had fled from his son, Absolom, St. Chrysostom says (55, 35, 2): "Rulers erect images of victorious charioteers and athletes and erect slabs with inscriptions on them which tell of the victory, as a herald would proclaim it with his voice. Others again describe the praise of the victors in books and writings; and painters and sculptors and smiths and peoples and rulers and cities and countries admire the victors, but no one has ever painted a picture of one who flees from a contest."

Theodore is told (47, 290, 47) that the contest lasts but a short time, so that now is the accepted time. "This also is the work of the loving-kindness of God, that our struggles (ἀγῶνας) are not protracted to a great length, but that after struggling (ἀγωνισαμένους) for a brief and tiny twinkling of an eye (for such is the present life compared with the other) we receive crowns of victory for endless ages. And it will be no small affliction to the souls of those who are being punished at that time, to reflect that, when they had it in their power in the few days of this life to make all good, they neglected their opportunity and surrendered themselves to everlasting evil. And lest we should suffer this, let us rouse ourselves while it is the accepted time, while it is the day of salvation [II Cor. VI, 2], while the power of repentance is great." The short duration of the contest is mentioned in 53, 76, 2, and is so applied to virginity in 53, 341, 4.

The two sons of Zebedee are informed that the present is not the season for rewards, but for conflicts. St. Matt. XX, 22: ". . . Are ye able to drink of the cup that I am about to drink of [and to be baptized with the baptism that I am baptized with]?" 58, 619, 42: "Do you see how He straightway drew them off from their suspicion, by framing His discourse from the contrary topics? 'For you,' He says, 'talk to me of honor and crowns, but I to you of conflicts (ἀγώνων) and labors.' For this is not the season for rewards (ἐπά-θλων)." This idea of the present being the time for contest and the rewards to come later is also found in 53, 49, 52; 54, 471, 36; *ib*. 567, 46; 55, 92, 48; *ib*. 127, 33.

Our whole life must be a scene of conflicts. The reference is to II Cor. I, 10: ". . . on whom we have set our hope that he will also still deliver us." 61, 396, 21: "Paul calls their prayers a great protection, at the same time showing that [this] our life must be throughout a scene of conflict (ἐναγώνιον), for he predicts many trials."

The fervent soul of Paul chose a life of conflict when he went away into Arabia. 61, 630, 34: "Behold a fervent soul! . . . He straightway undertook to teach wild barbarians, choosing a life full of conflict (βίον ἐναγώνιον) and labor."

We must be always prepared for conflict. 63, 478, 10: "We must live the present life ever prepared for conflict (ἐναγωνίους), in order that by laboring a little time we may be crowned forever."

The just man, like the athlete, must bear the contest of the present life nobly. 63, 879, 14: "I beseech you, brethren, to consider the forethought of God not only in respect of things present, but also of things to come. For the things present are a contest, a place of struggle and a stadium (ἀγὼν καὶ σκάμματα καὶ στάδιον). But the things to come are the rewards, crowns and prizes (ἔπαθλα καὶ στέφανοι καὶ βραβεῖα). Therefore just as it is necessary for the athlete in the lists (σκάμματι) to contend with sweat and dust and much heat and labors and suffering, even so must the just man here endure many things and bear all nobly, if he is going to receive the brilliant crowns there."

Nobility in the contest of the present life is shown by Abraham in respect to Sarah (53, 356, 44), where he weaves crowns for himself on all sides by allowing Sarah to deal with Hagar as she pleases, since Hagar, having conceived, is holding Sarah in contempt. Abraham still further displays the nobility of his character in the contest of sacrificing Isaac. 54, 430, 15: "When he knew the magnitude of the contest, he did not impart the knowledge of it to any one, not even to the servants or to Isaac himself, but endured the contest (ἀγῶνα ἠγωνίζετο) alone by himself and remained invincible (ἀκαταγώνιστος) as adamant, thus showing the strength of his mind in yielding to the will of God." For exercising this obedience and showing the devotion of his mind and will, Abraham receives the crown in 54, 432, 17; *ib.* 434, 37; *ib.* 444, 24.

It should be borne in mind that the present contest may terminate all too soon. 63, 899, 15: "A day will come when the theatre of this life will be concluded and no one will contend (ἀγωνίζεται) any longer. This is the season for repentance, that for crowns."

The Christian Contest is so serious that all that is superfluous should be discarded. Women may well dispense with their garments of silk. 63, 199, 12: "A woman who professes godliness can beautify herself in a far better way than those who adorn themselves on the stage. You also have a theatre which is heaven, the company of angels. . . . For in that place is no need of these garments of gold, . . . so as to make the body white and glistering, but so as to beautify the soul. For the soul it is, which is contending and wrestling (ἀγωνιζομένη καὶ ἀθλοῦσα) in that theatre."

True striving means earnestness to the extent of trembling and fearing, as in the case of Epaphras who was always striving in his prayers. 62, 381, 9: "He said not simply 'praying,' but 'striving (ἀγωνιζόμενος),' trembling and fearing."

St. Chrysostom recognizes the full force of striving in his brief comment on I Thess. II, 2: ". . . we waxed bold in our God to speak unto you the gospel of God in much conflict (πολλῷ ἀγῶνι)." 62, 401, 22: " 'You know full well,' he says, 'how great was our danger and how much contention (ἀγωνίας) we had when we were among you.' "

The exposition of St. Peter's restoration of Tabitha to life discovers that death is a release of the soul from a contest. 60, 168, 38: "The soul comes off as from a contest (ἀγῶνος) and goes to a very different light from that of this world."

The death of one in a monastery was celebrated with much joy, as the departed had successfully terminated his contest. 62, 577, 44: "When it is reported that any one is dead, then there is thanksgiving and great glory and joy, every one praying that such may be his own end, that so his own combat (ἀγῶνα) may terminate, that he may rest from his labor and struggles (ἀγώνων) and that he may see Christ."

Weariness should not cause a man to fall near the end of the contest. This opinion is in the interpretation of Heb. IV, 11: "Let us therefore give diligence to enter into that rest, that no man fall after the same example of disobedience." 63, 62, 10: "For that these also [to whom he is writing] had suffered much, he afterward testifies, saying, 'Call to remembrance the former days, in which, after ye were enlightened, ye endured a great conflict (ἄθλησιν) of sufferings [Heb. X, 32].' Let no man then be faint-hearted or fall near the end through weariness. For there are those who at the beginning engage in the fight (ἀγῶνας) with the full vigor of zeal, but a little after, not being willing to add to all, they lose all."

In virtue there must be an end suitable to the beginning, else everything is undone. The reference is to Heb. XI, 13: ". . . having confessed that they were strangers and pilgrims on the earth." 63, 170, 10: "Let us also, my beloved, become 'strangers,' that God may not be ashamed of us. . . . For not only ought we to have our beginnings splendid, but the end also more splendid still. . . . If the athlete makes not a more splendid display and conquers to the end and if after vanquishing all he is vanquished by the last, is not all unprofitable to him? . . . . So too in respect of virtue, as many as have not added an end suitable to the beginning, are ruined and undone. Such are they who have sprung forth (προπηδήσαντες) from the starting-place (βαλβίδων), bright and exulting, and afterward have become faint and feeble. Therefore they both are deprived of the prize (βραβείου) and are not acknowledged by their Master."

There must be a contest to the very end in fasting. 56, 139, 19: "Even as in the Olympic games the end of the wrestlings is the crown, so the end of fasting is pure communion. Unless we are set right through these days, we have contended in vain and we depart uncrowned and without prizes (βραβείων) from the contest (σκάμματος) of fasting."

There is more remissness on the part of Christians than there should be with regard to the heavenly contest. 60, 660, 24: "Men that lead the populace, if they have but common matters to deliberate, add days to nights in watching. And we who are struggling (τὸν ἀγῶνα ἔχοντες) in heaven's behalf sleep even in the daytime."

The Christian, like St. Paul, will do more than is necessary, as he says in II Cor. I, 12: ". . . in the grace of God, we behaved ourselves (ἀνεστράφημεν) in the world, and more abundantly to you-ward." 61, 406, 21: "Paul says that we showed both signs and wonders among you, and greater strictness (ἀκρίβειαν) and a life unblameable; for he calls these, too, the grace of God, ascribing his own good works also to it. For in Corinth he even overleaped the goal (τὰ σκάμματα ὑπερέβη), making the gospel without charge, because he spared their weakness."

St. Paul's example of unremitting zeal is again mentioned in the comment on Phil. I, 24: ". . . to abide in the flesh is more needful for your sake." 62, 207, 16: "What excuse shall we have, when Paul still remained in the contest (ἀγωνιζόμενος) on behalf of man?"

The disciples in renouncing themselves should enter themselves in all contests, that they may win the crown because of their own exertion. 58, 542, 10: "Christ said not, 'Let him not spare himself,' but, very strictly, 'Let him renounce himself;' that is, let him have nothing to do with himself, but expose himself to all dangers and conflicts (ἀγῶσι); and let him so feel, as if another should be suffering it all. And He said not, 'Let him deny (ἀρνησάσθω),' but 'Let him renounce (ἀπαρνησάσθω);' even by this small addition intimating again how very far it goes. For this latter is more than the former. . . . Ib. 541, 34: 'You have need of many toils, many dangers, if you are to come after me. For you ought not, O Peter, because you have confessed me Son of God, therefore only to expect crowns and to suppose this enough for your salvation and for the future to enjoy security, as having done all'. . . For so, if one should be a judge in the games (ἀγωνοθέτης) and should have a friend (φίλον ἀθλητήν) in the lists, he would not wish to crown him by favor only, but also for his own toils; and for this reason especially, because he loves him. Even so Christ also; whom He most loves, those He most of all will have to approve themselves by their own means also, and not from His help alone."

The Christian Athlete must always keep his mind in the best of condition. 62, 263, 24: "In our contests (ἀγῶσιν) with heretics we must make the attack with minds in full vigor (ἀκμαζούσαις), that they may be able to give exact attention."

God does not refuse help to the one who is struggling in the contest. St. Chrysostom mentions this in speaking of the imperishable crowns which Abraham won. 54, 385, 54: "When He, who knows the secrets of our hearts, sees us eagerly prepare for contests (ἀγῶνας) of virtue, He instantly supplies us with His assistance, lightening our labors and strengthening the weakness of our nature. In the Olympic games the trainer (παιδοτρίβης) stands by as a spectator merely, awaiting the issue and unable to contribute anything to the efforts of the contender; whereas our Master aids us (συναγωνίζεται), extends his hand to us, all but subdues our antagonist (ἀντίπαλον), arranges everything to enable us to prevail, that He may place the amaranthine wreath upon our brows."

The contest has been made easier by the Spirit. This occurs in the exegesis of II Cor. III, 7, 8: "But if the ministration of death, written, and engraven on stones, came with glory, so that the children of Israel could not look stedfastly upon the face of Moses for the glory of his face; which glory was passing away: how shall not rather the ministration of the spirit be with glory?" 61, 442, 47: "See how he [Paul] cuts at the root of the Jewish arrogancy. For the law was nothing else but letters: a certain succor was not found leaping forth (ἐκπηδῶσα) from out the letters and inspiring those who combat (ἀγωνιζομένοις), as in the case of baptism."

The Spirit enables the one who now contends to win the prizes easily (II Cor. VI, 2: ". . . behold, now is the acceptable time . . ."). 61, 482, 33: "While then we are yet in the lists (ἐν τῷ σκάμματι), let us draw nigh and show forth life; for it is also easy. For he who strives for the mastery (ἀγωνιζόμενος) at such a time, when so great a gift has been shed forth, when so great grace, will easily obtain the prizes (βραβείων)."

The true athlete will give encouragement to others, even though he endures great tribulation at the time (Col. IV, 3: ". . . praying for us also, that God may open unto us a door for the word, to speak the mystery of Christ, for which I am also in bonds"). 62, 369, 18: "The great athlete said not, 'That I may be freed from my bonds,' but being in bonds he exhorted others,—and exhorted them for a great object, that he himself might get boldness in speaking."

St. Paul also raises the Philippians in Phil. I, 30: "having the same conflict (ἀγῶνα) which ye saw in me. . . ." 62, 209, 22: "Here again he raises them, by showing them that everywhere their conflicts (ἀγωνιζομένους) are the same with his, that their struggles (ἀθλοῦν-τας) are the same with his, both severally and in that they unite with him in bearing trials. . . . See you the praises of the men of that time? But we endure not so much as buffetings or blows, neither insult nor loss of our possessions; they were straightway zealous and all of them strove (ἦσαν ἀγωνιζόμενοι) as martyrs, while we have grown cold in love toward Christ."

St. Paul gives encouragement in Col. III, 15: "And let the peace of Christ rule (βραβευέτω) in your hearts . . . and be ye thankful." 62, 360, 31: "And whatsoever our sufferings may be, let us think upon things yet more fearful, and we shall have comfort sufficient. . . . So Paul also exhorts us; as when he says, 'Ye have not yet resisted unto blood, striving against (ἀνταγωνιζόμενοι) sin [Heb. XII, 4].'"

St. Paul's words give cheer in Col. IV, 18: ". . . Remember my bonds. . . ." 62, 382, 14: "Wonderful! How great the consolation! For this is enough to cheer them on to all things and to make them bear themselves more nobly in their contests (ἀγῶνας)."

Encouragement as to the end of the contest is given in Heb. I, 1, 2: "God . . . hath at the end of these days spoken unto us in his Son . . . ." 63, 14, 51: "For as Paul says also in another place, 'For now is salvation nearer to us than when we first believed [Rom. XIII, 11].' What then is it which he says?—that whoever is spent (κατανωθείς) in the conflict (ἀγῶνι), when he hears of the end thereof, recovers his breath a little, knowing that it is the end indeed of his labors and the beginning of his rest (ἀναπαύσεως)."

St. Paul ever striving in the contest still feels the need of the prayers of others, as in Phil. I, 19: ". . . this shall turn out to my salvation, through your supplication. . . ." 62, 198, 39: "Behold the humble-mindedness of this blessed one: he was striving in the contest (ἐν τοῖς ἄθλοις ἦν ἀγωνιζόμενος), he was now close to his crown, he had done ten thousand exploits, for he was Paul; and what can one add to this? Still he writes to the Philippians, 'I may be saved through your supplication.'"

The Christian Athlete looks only to God as the spectator of his actions. 62, 674, 22: "Lift up your thoughts to the theatre above. When in doing any good you consider that it ought to be displayed to men and you seek for some spectators of the action, reflect that God beholds you, and all that desire will be extinguished. Retire from the earth, and look to that theatre which is in heaven."

Exhortation is also given to think of God in 56, 102, 58. St. Chrysostom is here speaking to those who attend the amusements of the world which are far from edifying, and he draws a picture of all the prophets and teachers pointing to the Lord of angels sitting on his high and lofty throne distributing prizes (βραβεῖα) and crowns to those who are worthy, but assigning Gehenna and fire to those who are not worthy.

The heavenly spectators should be remembered, when one is treated unjustly in this world (St. John XVIII, 36: "Jesus answered, My kingdom is not of this world. . . ."). 59, 454, 4: "If a man has insulted you unjustly, in this case surely you ought not to grieve at all, but to pity him; . . . and delight yourself in the theatre of heaven. For there all will praise and applaud and welcome you. For one angel is as good as all the world. But why speak I of angels, when the Lord Himself shall proclaim (ἀνακηρύξει) you? Let us exercise ourselves (γυμνάζωμεν) with these reasonings."

The Christian Athlete shows his freedom from vainglory by not rushing into contests unnecessarily. Such is the comment on St. Matt. VI, 13: "And bring us not into temptation, but deliver us from the evil one [for thine is the kingdom, and the power, and the glory, for ever]." 57, 282, 5: "Here He quells our pride, instructing us to deprecate all conflicts (ἀγῶνας) instead of rushing upon (ἐπιπηδᾶν) them. For so both our victory will be more glorious and the devil's overthrow more derisive. I mean, that, as when we are dragged forth (ἑλκυσθέντας), we must stand nobly; so when we are not summoned, we should be quiet and wait for the time of conflict (ἀγώνων), that we may show both freedom from vainglory and nobility of spirit."

The courageous athlete is temperate and mild. 61, 151, 16: "The Three Children [Shadrach, Meshach and Abednego] entered into the fire and they neither cast insult upon the king nor overturned the statue.[1] The courageous man should be temperate and mild,—and that especially in dangers, that he may not seem to go forth to such contests (ἀγῶνας) in wrath and vainglory, but with fortitude and self-possession. . . . He who endures and is forced into the struggle (ἀγωνιζόμενος) and goes through the trial with meekness is not only admired as brave, but his self-possession also and consideration cause him to be no less extolled."

A distinction is made between boldness and forwardness in the Christian Contest. 60, 336, 30: "What is boldness?—when others are the persons for whom we contend (ἀγωνιζώμεθα). What is forwardness?—when it is in our own cause that we are willing to fight. Therefore magnanimity and boldness go together, as also [mere] forwardness and [mere] cowardice. . . . It betokens great strength, this gentleness; it needs a generous and a gallant soul and one of exceeding loftiness, this gentleness."

The idea as to how general our struggle should be in contending for others is briefly stated in the comment on I Cor. V, 6: ". . . Know ye not that a little leaven leaveneth the whole lump?" 61, 124, 51: "In these words Paul indicates that our struggle (ἀγών) is for the whole Church, and not for any one person."

However, the cause of religion finally recalls St. Chrysostom to the contest. 64, 472, 46: "I wished to be separated from you only for a short time; . . . but the cause of religion calls me to the com-

---

[1]This may be a covert allusion to the outrage on the statues of Theodosius, which had brought Antioch into so great trouble in 387, while St. Chrysostom was resident there.

bat (ἀγῶνας); and I must run to the lists (σκάμματα) of the Church, having received prayers which are helpful in the work."

St. Paul was the exemplary Christian athlete who took part in every form of contest. 61, 573, 21: "He was like some champion (ἀθλητής) who wrestles, runs and boxes (παλαίων, τρέχων, πυκτεύων)."

St. Paul's athletic prowess is emphasized in the treatise *De Sacerdotio* (48, 668, 44), where the priests of the present time are compared with St. Paul. "But the men of to-day—not that I would say anything harsh or severe, for indeed I do not speak by way of insult to them, but only in wonder—how is it that they do not shudder when they measure themselves with so great a man as this? For if we leave the miracles and turn to the life of this blessed saint and look into his angelic conversation, it is in this rather than in his miracles that you will find this Christian athlete a conqueror. For how can one describe his zeal and forbearance, his constant perils, his continual cares and incessant anxiety for the churches, his sympathy with the weak, his many afflictions, his unwonted persecutions, his deaths daily? Where is the spot in the world, where is the continent or sea, that is a stranger to the contests (ἄθλους) of this righteous man? Even the desert has known his presence, for it often sheltered him in time of danger. For he underwent every species of attack and achieved every kind of victory, and there was never any end to his contests and his crowns (καὶ οὔτε ἀγωνιζόμενος, οὔτε στεφανούμενος διέλιπέ ποτε)."

PART III. THE PRIZES

The Christian contest is different from the Olympic games in respect to prizes, since everyone is successful; the only difference is that one person may obtain a more splendid proclamation than another. 47, 382, 57: "He who desires something puts no hindrances in the way, but does all that it may come to pass. Yea, for those who go into the Olympic games know that in such a large number there will be but one victor, yet they strive and suffer blows. However, the ratio is not the same here as there, not only on account of the issue of the contests (ἀγώνων), but also because there of necessity only one goes away crowned; while here there is no superiority in one going away crowned or inferiority in one going away uncrowned, but all meet with success: one obtaining a more splendid proclamation (ἀνακηρύξεως), the other a lesser."

The certainty that God will not be remiss in rewarding His athletes occurs also in 57, 215, 57. "Will God overlook and leave uncrowned His own servants, Peter and Paul and James and John, those who every day for His sake suffered hunger, were bound, were scourged, were drowned in the sea, were given up to wild beasts, were dying, were suffering so great things as we cannot so much as reckon? And whereas the judge (ἀγωνοθέτης) proclaims and crowns the Olympic victor (τὸν 'Ολυμπιονίκην), and the king rewards the soldier, . . . shall God alone, after those so great toils and labors, repay them with no good thing great or small?"

Assurance of prizes such as come by faith is based on Heb. XI, 20: "By faith Isaac blessed Jacob and Esau, even concerning things to come." 63, 179, 12: "Some of the things here are examples of patience only and of enduring ill-treatment and of receiving nothing good: for instance, what is mentioned in the case of Abraham. But others are examples of faith, as in the case of Noah, that there is a God, that there is a recompense. For faith in this place is manifold, both of there being a recompense and of awaiting it, not under the same conditions, and of contending (ἀθλεῖν) before the prizes (ἐπάθλων)."

The nature of the heavenly crown is shown in 58, 638, 51. "For toil upon worldly matters everywhere bears not fruit; nay, but even, when it has not failed, but has brought forth its produce even abundantly, short is the time wherein it continues. For when you are grown old and have no longer afterward the feeling of enjoyment in perfection, then and not till then, does the labor bear you its recompense. And whereas the labor was with the body in its vigor, the fruit and the enjoyment is with one grown old and languid, when time has dulled even the feeling, although, if it has not dulled it, the expectation of the end suffers us not to find pleasure. But in the other case not so; the labor is in corruption and a dying body, but the crown in one [body] incorruptible and immortal and having no end. And the labor is both first and short-lived, but the reward both subsequent and endless, that with security you may take your rest after that, looking for nothing unpleasant. For neither may you fear change any more nor loss as here. What sort of good things, then, are these, which are both insecure and short-lived and earthly and vanishing before they have appeared and acquired with many toils? And what good things are equal to those, that are immovable, that grow not old, that have no toil, that even at the time of the conflicts (ἀγώνων) bring you crowns?"

Those who were more glorious in their dangers received the more brilliant crowns. 57, 192, 14: "When Paul sought to be delivered from the temptation ('a thorn in the flesh, a messenger of Satan to buffet me [II Cor. XII, 7]'), he obtained it not by reason of the great benefit ensuing. And if we should go over the whole life of David, we shall find him more glorious in his dangers,—both himself and all the others that were like him. For so Job at that season shone forth the more abundantly, and Joseph too in this way became the more approved, and his father's father,—and all as many as ever put on crowns of peculiar glory (λαμπροτέρους στεφάνους); it was by tribulations and temptations that they first won their crowns and then had their names recited (ἀνεκηρύχθησαν)." The same is said of the athlete Joseph (54, 529, 33), when he is ill-treated by his brethren, and also (ib. 543, 34), when he is forgotten in prison by the butler.

St. Paul's enemies make his crown brilliant by binding him. This arises from the comment on Col. IV, 3: ". . . to speak the mystery of Christ, for which I am also in bonds." 62, 371, 11: "He was both more tenderly regretted by his friends and more reverenced by his enemies, as bearing the prize (ἔπαθλον) for courage in his bonds. And a crown binds the head; but it disgraces it not, yea rather, it makes it brilliant. Against their wills they crowned him with his chain."

If we do not recover our losses in this life, our reward hereafter will be greater. 63, 147, 7: "The devil causes us losses, not that he may take away our goods only (for he knows that is nothing), but that through them he may compel us to utter some blasphemy. . . . If then we bear losses thankfully, we shall recover even these things; and if we shall not recover them, our reward will be greater. For when Job had wrestled (ἤθλησε) nobly, then God restored to him these things also."

A fitting exegesis is made of Heb. XI, 13, 16 on the prizes which those will receive who have labored in God's behalf. "These all died in faith, not having received the promises, but having seen them and greeted them from afar, . . . for he [God] hath prepared for them a city." 63, 163, 47: "Of what kind are those good things likely to be, of which God is the preparer and establisher? For if immediately after He had made us, when we had not yet done anything, He freely bestowed so great favors: paradise, familiar intercourse with Himself, promise of immortality, of a life happy and freed from cares,—what will He not bestow on those who have labored and struggled so greatly (ἠθληκόσι) and endured on His behalf?"

Prizes are always mentioned in connection with the Christian contest. 57, 272, 20: "And this most especially we may admire in Christ's teaching, that, while in each instance He sets down with very great fullness the prizes of the conflicts (τὰ ἔπαθλα τῶν ἀγώνων): such as 'to see God' and 'to inherit the kingdom of heaven' and 'to become sons of God' and 'like God' and 'to obtain mercy' and 'to be comforted' and 'the great reward', if anywhere He must needs mention grievous conflicts (e. g., loving one's enemies), He does this in a subdued tone. He corrects the hearer rather in the way of shaming than threatening him where He says, 'Do not even the publicans the same [St. Matt. V, 1–12, 46]?'"

Prizes are also found in the exposition of St. Matt. XVI, 27: "For the Son of man shall come in the glory of his Father with his angels; and then he shall render unto every man according to his deeds." 58, 545, 12: "He suffered not however His discourse to appear only dismal, but tempered it also with good hopes. Nor did He say, 'Then shall He punish those who sinned,' but 'He shall reward every man according to his doings.' And this He said, reminding not only the sinners of punishment, but also those who have done well of prizes (βραβείων) and crowns."

Christ may set forth the prize even before the contest is mentioned, as he did to the young man who says in St. Matt. XIX, 20: ". . . All these things have I observed: what lack I yet?" 58, 604, 51: "What then said Christ? Since He was going to enjoin something great, He set forth the rewards (ἔπαθλα) and said, 'If thou wouldest be perfect, go, sell that which thou hast, and give to the poor, and thou shalt have treasure in heaven: and come, follow me.' See you how many prizes (βραβεῖα), how many crowns, He appoints for this race (σταδίῳ)? .... Even before mentioning the conflict (ἀγῶνα) and the toil, He shows him the prize (βραβεῖον), saying, 'If thou wouldest be perfect,' and then says, 'Sell that which thou hast, and give to the poor,' and straightway again the rewards (ἔπαθλα), 'Thou shalt have treasure in heaven: and come, follow me.' For indeed to follow Him is a great recompense. 'And thou shalt have treasure in heaven.' "

The prize is set forth in St. John VI, 27: "Work not for the food which perisheth, but for the food which abideth unto eternal life . . . ." 59, 251, 20: "He set before them the prize (ἔπαθλον), saying, 'But that which abideth unto eternal life.' "

The prize is mentioned together with the contest in St. John XII, 26: "If any man serve me, let him follow me; and where I am, there shall also my servant be . . . ." 59, 371, 13: "Then after He had spoken what was hard to bear, He put also the prize (ἔπαθλον). And of what kind was this? The following Him and being where He is, showing that resurrection shall succeed death."

There is a great reward not only for those who incur dangers, but also for those who suffer calumny. 57, 230, 9: "It is hardest to bear the revilings of men, when they say all manner of evil against us. For whereas in our dangers there are many things that lighten the toil, as to be anointed (ἀλείφεσθαι) by all, to have many to applaud (κροτοῦντας), to crown, to proclaim our praise (ἀνακηρύττοντας); here in our reproach even this consolation is destroyed. For it would seem that we have not achieved anything great; and this galls the combatant (δάκνει τὸν ἀγωνιζόμενον) more than all his dangers. . . . But Paul proclaims the triumph of these also, thus saying, 'Call to remembrance the former days, in which, after ye were enlightened, ye endured a great conflict of sufferings; partly, being made a gazing-stock both by reproaches and afflictions [Heb. X, 32, 33].' On this account then Christ has appointed the reward also to be great."

The value of the heavenly rewards as to bearing the contest easily is made in the comment on St. Matt. VII, 14: "For narrow is the gate, and straitened the way, that leadeth unto life, and few are they that find it." 57, 314, 37: "The part of virtue becomes easier in the end. For not the passing away of our labors and our toils, but their issuing in a good end (for they end in life) is enough to console those in conflict (ἀγωνιζομένους). So that both the temporary nature of our labors and the perpetuity of our crowns and the fact that the labors come first and the crowns after must prove a very great relief in our toils. Wherefore Paul also called their affliction 'light', not from the nature of the events, but because of the mind of the combatants (ἀγωνιζομένων) and the hope of the future. 'For our light affliction,' says he, 'worketh an eternal weight of glory; while we look not at the things which are seen, but at the things which are not seen [II Cor. IV, 17, 18].' . . . . For if to boxers (τοῖς πυκτεύουσιν) the sharp blows (δριμεῖαι πληγαί) are light and tolerable things, all of them, for the hope of those rewards (ἐπάθλων) which are temporary and perishing, much more when heaven is set forth and the unspeakable blessings and the eternal rewards (τὰ ἀθάνατα ἔπαθλα), will no one feel any of the present hardships. . . . See how He on another side also makes it easy, commanding us to 'beware of the false prophets;' thus causing men to feel as if in real conflict (ἐναγωνίους). And the very fact, too, of calling it 'narrow' contributed very greatly toward making it easy; for it wrought on them to be vigilant, as Paul, when he says, 'Our wrestling is not against flesh and blood [Eph. VI, 12].' . . . Consider not that the way is strait and narrow, but where it ends. Christ says this to awaken our alacrity. For whoever is in conflict (ἀγωνιζόμενος), when he actually sees the judge of the lists (ἀγωνοθέτην) marvelling at the painfullness of his efforts (ἀγωνισμάτων), is the more inspirited."

By looking to the rewards it will be easy to do the Lord's will. 58, 539, 31: "What is the Lord's will? It is, 'Impart to the neighbors, share your bread, cancel the contracts unjustly made.' What is more easy than this? Tell me. But even if you account it difficult, look, I pray you, at the rewards (ἔπαθλα) also, and it shall be easy for you. For much as our emperors at the chariot-races (ἱπποδρομίαις) heap together before the combatants (ἀγωνιζομένων) crowns and prizes (βραβεῖα) and garments, even so Christ also sets His rewards (ἔπαθλα) in the midst of His course (σταδίῳ), holding them out by the prophet's words, as it were by both hands. And the emperors, although being ten thousand times emperors, yet being men, and having their wealth in a course of spending and their munificence of exhaustion, are ambitious of making a little appear much; wherefore also they commit each thing severally into the hand of the several attendants and so bring it forward. But our King contrariwise, having heaped all together (because He is very rich and does nothing for display), He so brings it forward, and what

He so reaches out is indefinitely great, and will need many hands to hold it. 'Then,' says he, 'shall thy light break forth as the morning [Is. LVIII, 8].' Does not this gift appear to you as some one thing? But it is not; nay, for it has many things in it, both prizes (βραβεῖα) and crowns and other rewards (ἔπαθλα)."

By looking to the delight which the crown gives, the athlete is enabled to undergo the contest with pleasure. This is based on II Cor. VI, 10: "as sorrowful, yet always rejoicing. . . ." 61, 486, 25: "The faithful only are right judges of these matters and are not pleased and pained at the same things as other people. For if anyone who knew nothing of the games (ἀγώνων) should see a boxer (πυκτεύοντα) having wounds upon him and wearing a crown, he would think him in pain on account of the wounds, not understanding the pleasure the crown would give him. And these therefore, because they know what we suffer, but do not know for what we suffer them, naturally suspect that there is nought besides them; for they see indeed the wrestlings (παλαίσματα) and the dangers, but not the prizes (ἔπαθλα) and the crowns and the object of the contest (ὑπόθεσιν τῶν ἀγώνων). . . . In every kind of virtue compute not only the severity of the toils, but also the sweetness of the prizes (ἐπάθλων), and before all the subject of this wrestling, our Lord Jesus; and you will readily enter upon the contest (ἀγώνων) and will live the whole time in pleasure. For nothing is so wont to cause pleasure as a good conscience."

Constant thought of the crowns and applause which come from the heavenly theatre will do away with the mad desire for glory which is the cause of all evils. 59, 172, 5: "Now if you look to that theatre, learn what crowns are there, transport yourself into the applause which comes thence, never will earthly things be able to hold you; neither when they come will you deem them great nor when they are away seek after them."

Consideration of the future crowns also occurs in 59, 414, 34. "Considering the crowns twined for us after the conflicts (ἀγώνων), let us admire not wealth and honor and luxury and power, but poverty and the chain and bonds and endurance in the cause of virtue."

Thought of the crown makes an easy struggle in the case of a "strange woman." 59, 418, 34: "When it is hard to despise the love of a 'strange woman,' think of the crown which comes after the struggle, and you shall easily bear the struggle. . . . Indeed those who are virtuous, even apart from the promises of things to come, think it a great thing to be sober-minded, because God has commanded it. But if any one is too weak for this, let him think of the prizes (βραβεῖα).''

There are prizes for us to consider in the comment on Heb. XII, 2: ''. . . who for the joy that was set before him endured the cross. . . . and hath sat down at the right hand of the throne of God.'' 63, 194, 8: ''If then He, who was under no necessity of being crucified, was crucified for our sake, how much more is it right that we should endure all things nobly? . . . . What then is the end? 'He is set down at the right hand of the throne of God.' See you the prize (ἔπαθλον)? . . . . Even if there should be no prize, the example would suffice to persuade us to accept all [such] things. But now prizes (ἔπαθλα) also are set before us,—and these no common ones, but great and unspeakable.''

The crown may be lost for want of a slight endeavor. This interpretation is made on St. Matt. XXIV, 16, 17: ''then let them that are in Judaea flee into the mountains: let him that is on the housetop not go down to take out the things that are in his house.'' 58, 699, 35: ''We lose heaven for want of a slight endeavor. For both the time is short and the labor small, and yet we faint and are supine. You strive (ἀγωνίζει) on earth, and the crown is in heaven; . . . the race is for two days and the reward (βραβεῖα) for endless ages; the struggle (πάλη) is a corruptible body and the rewards incorruptible. . . . Earthly things must be surrendered because you are mortal; He wills you to do this by your choice, which you must do by necessity. So much only He requires to be added, that it should be done for His sake. See you how easy is the conflict (ἀγών)? . . . . We neglect the simple and easy things of God which are of infinite worth, and hasten away to fighting and wars and wild struggles (παγκράτια) and trials and suits of law. . . . Why do you turn away from Him who loves you? Why do you labor for the world and for the present life? Why do you 'beat (πυκτεύεις) the air'? Why do you 'run in vain'?''

God rewards us even before our struggles,—and this is all the greater reason why He will give us great crowns afterward. 60, 470, 19: ''If He had not been willing to present us after our labors with great crowns, He would never have given us such mighty gifts [the Holy Spirit] before our labors. But now the warmth of His love is hence made apparent, that it is not gradually and little by little that He honors us, but He has shed abroad the full fountain of His blessings,—and this too before our struggles (ἀγώνων).'' Crowns are also given before the contest to those who exercise self-control in 56, 291, 26.

The difference between rewards as under grace and under the law is further emphasized in reference to Rom. VI, 14: "For sin shall not have dominion over you: for ye are not under the law, but under grace." 60, 488, 17: "It is not the law only that exhorts us, but grace, too, which also remits our former sins and secures us against future ones. For it promised them crowns after toils, but this [*i.e.*, grace] crowned them first and then led them to the contest (εἰς τοὺς ἀγῶνας εἵλκυσιν)."

Grace crowns us at the outset. The comment is on Rom. VIII, 2: "For the law of the Spirit of life in Christ Jesus made me free from the law of sin and of death." 60, 513, 31: "The grace of the Spirit has freed us from the law of sin and made the contest (ἀγῶνα) light to us, crowning us at the outset and then drawing us to the struggles (ἐπὶ τὰ παλαίσματα ἑλκύσασα) with abundant help."

The man who is addicted to lust may win the prize before his struggle. 60, 505, 55: "Are you lustful (λάγνος) and dissipated? Make it your rule again not even to look at a woman or to go into the theatre or to trouble yourself with the beauty of other people. It is far easier not even to look at a woman of good figure than, after looking and taking in the lust, to thrust out the perturbation that comes thereof, the struggle (ἀγῶνες) being easier in the preliminaries. ... What need to have superfluous trouble, when before the wrestling (πάλης) you may seize upon the prize (βραβεῖον)?"

We also have another crown while here in life, according to the remarks on Rom. VI, 8: "But if we died with Christ . . . ." 60, 485, 41: "And indeed even before the crown, this is in itself the greater crown: the partaking of death with our Master. But He says, 'I give you even another reward (ἔπαθλον): it is life eternal.'"

The rewards are appointed even now when the labor is mentioned, as in St. Matt. XI, 29, 30: "Take my yoke upon you, and learn of me; for I am meek and lowly in heart: and ye shall find rest unto your souls. For my yoke is easy, and my burden is light." 57, 431, 21: "If you duly perform His words, by becoming lowly and meek and gentle, the burden will be light. And exceeding great is the reward (ἔπαθλον) which He appoints. 'For not to another only do you become serviceable, but yourself also above all you refresh,' says He. For 'ye shall find rest unto your souls [St. Matt. XI, 29].' Even before the things to come, He gives you here your recompense and bestows the prize (βραβεῖον) already, making the saying acceptable both hereby and by setting Himself forward as an example."

The Christian struggles have a relish in themselves, so that we have the prizes during the contest. The comment is on Rom. V, 3: ". . . we also rejoice in our tribulations." 60, 469, 14: "In the case of external things the struggles (ἀγῶνες) for them bring trouble and pain and irksomeness along with them; and it is the crowns and rewards (ἔπαθλα) that carry the pleasure with them. But in this case it is not so, for the wrestlings (παλαίσματα) have no less relish to us than the rewards. For since there were sundry temptations in those days and the kingdom existed in hopes (and this unnerved the feebler sort), therefore now even before the crowns He gives them the prize (βραβεῖα), saying that we should 'glory even in tribulations.'"

Conscience immediately crowns the man whose soul rejoices in doing what is right. Reference is made very fittingly to Col. III, 15: "And let the peace of Christ rule (βραβευέτω, 'act as umpire') in your hearts . . . and be ye thankful." 62, 357, 32: "A man who gives thanks for his evils is not sensible of them. For his soul rejoices, as doing what is right; and forthwith his conscience is bright and crowns and proclaims (ἀνακηρύττει) him."

Crowns are also given at the time of contest, in the interpretation of II Cor. I, 5: "For as the sufferings of Christ abound unto us, even so our comfort also aboundeth through Christ." 61, 387, 34: " 'Our comfort aboundeth,' so that the season of struggles (ἀγώνων) was the season also of fresh crowns."

A quite valid reason for the prizes being given after the conflict is observed on the text of I Cor. III, 13: "each man's work shall be made manifest . . . ." 61, 76, 33: "God promises us greater things than paradise, but He does not give them now lest He should unnerve (διαχέῃ) us in the season of conflicts (ἀγώνων); yet He has not been silent about the prizes, lest we should be quite cast down with our labors."

The idea of the rewards being given subsequent to the contest occurs in the exegesis of Acts XII, 19: "And when Herod had sought for him [Peter], and found him not, he examined the guards, and commanded that they should be put to death." 60, 203, 51: "Some persons, it is likely, are at a loss how to explain it, that God should quietly look on while His champions (ἀθλητάς) are put to death, and now again the soldiers on account of Peter; and yet it was possible for Him after delivering Peter to rescue them also. . . . But it was not yet the season of distribution, so as to render to each according to his deserts."

It is a higher distinction for the crown to be received not where the place of contest is, but to be called up and be crowned by the king above. This arises from the observation on Phil. III, 14: "I press on toward the goal unto the prize of the high calling of God in Christ Jesus." 62, 272, 13: "And what is this prize? No palm branch; but what? The kingdom of heaven, everlasting rest, glory together with Christ, the inheritance, brotherhood, ten thousand good things, which it is impossible to name. . . . Christ has willed that you should struggle (ἀγωνίζεσθαι) below, on high He crowns you. Not as in this world; the crown is not here, where the contest (ἀγών) is, but the crown is in that bright place. See you not even here that the most honored of the athletes and charioteers are not crowned in the course (σταδίῳ) below, but the king calls them up and crowns them there? Thus too is it here, in heaven you receive the prize (βραβεῖον)."

It is not a difficult matter to carry off the prize, as Christ indicates in St. Matt. XI, 30: "For my yoke is easy, and my burden is light." 57, 432, 25: "What is more grievous than to turn the cheek, and when smitten not to smite again? Yet nevertheless, if we practise self-command (φιλοσοφῶμεν), all these things are light and easy and pleasurable. . . . Again, to turn the cheek is, to him that gives heed, a less grievous thing than to smite another; for from this the contest has beginning, in that termination; and whereas by the latter you have kindled also the other's pile, by the former you have quenched even your own flames. But that not to be burnt is a pleasanter thing than to be burnt, is surely plain to every man. And if this holds in regard to bodies, much more so in regard to a soul. And which is lighter: to contend (ἀγωνίζεσθαι) or to be crowned? to fight (πυκτεύειν) or to have the prize (βραβεῖον)? Therefore, also, to die is better than to live. . . . And if you disbelieve our sayings, hearken to those who have seen the countenances of the martyrs in the time of their conflicts (ἀγώνων), how, when scourged and flayed, they were exceeding joyful and glad and, when exposed upon hot irons, rejoiced and were glad of heart, more than such as lie upon a bed of roses."

Evidence on prizes being won by suffering evil is clearly seen again in 61, 596, 8. "Let us not fear to suffer evil, but to do evil; for that indeed is victory, but this defeat. For by suffering evil come those crowns, those prizes (βραβεῖα), that proclamation of victory (ἀνακήρυξις). And this may be seen in all the saints who have been thus crowned and proclaimed (ἀνεκηρύχθησαν)."

The same sentiment on how to be proclaimed the victor is given in 59, 53, 6. "To suffer evil is to get the crown. If then we wish to be proclaimed victors by God, let us not in these contests (παλαίσμασι) observe the laws of the games, but those of God, to learn to bear all things with longsuffering; for so we may get the better of our antagonists (παλαιόντων) and obtain both present and promised good things."

Job's afflictions resulted in the best of rewards. 62, 642, 44: "His crowns were splendid, his prizes (βραβεῖα) glorious." Job also showed his perfect resignation as he endured the contest, knowing that he was worthy of the prizes. 64, 544, 2: "When Job saw his life and his conscience, which was brighter than the sun, and the multitude of his upright deeds, he knew that he was worthy of the crowns and prizes (βραβείων) and countless rewards (μυρίων ἐπάθλων). Yet when he saw that he was suffering heavier punishment than those who had committed the basest crimes, he said, 'As it pleased the Lord, so was it done; blessed be the name of Jehovah [Job I, 21]!'"

A glorious victory is depicted in the description of a Christian burial, 63, 43, 4. The scene is based on Heb. II, 15: "and might deliver all them who through fear of death were all their lifetime subject to bondage." "What mean the bright torches? Do we not send them [the departed ones] before as athletes? And what mean the hymns? Do we not glorify God and give thanks that at last He has crowned the departed one, that He has freed him from his labors?"

We are immortal because of our victory over death. The thought arises from St. John XVI, 33: "These things have I spoken unto you, that in me ye may have peace. . . ." 59, 429, 29: "Death shall not gain the mastery over us. The champion (ἀνταγωνιστής) truly will then be glorious, not when he has not closed with (συμπλακῇ) his opponent, but when having closed he is not holden by him. We therefore are not mortal because of our struggle (συμπλοκήν) with death, but immortal because of our victory."

The nature of a glorious victory is made quite plain in the comment on St. Matt. XXVI, 51, 52: ". . . one of them that were with Jesus stretched out his hand, and drew his sword, and smote the servant of the high priest, and struck off his ear. Then saith Jesus unto him, Put up again thy sword into its place: for all they that take the sword shall perish with the sword." 58, 756, 29: "Nowhere do we overcome by doing wrongfully, but everywhere by suffering wrong-

fully. Thus also does the victory become more glorious, when we
sufferers get the better of the doers. Hereby it is shown that the
victory is of God. For indeed it has an opposite nature to outward
conquest, which fact is again above all an infallible sign of strength.
Thus also the rocks in the sea, by being struck, break the waves;
thus also all the saints were proclaimed (ἀνεκηρύχθησαν) and crowned
and erected their glorious trophies, winning this tranquil victory. 'For
stir not yourself,' He says, 'nor weary yourself. God has given you
this might, to conquer not by conflict (συμπλοκῆς), but by endurance
alone. Do not oppose yourself also as he does, and you have conquered; conflict (συμπλακῆς) not, and you have gained the crown.
Why do you disgrace yourself? Allow him not to say that by con-
flicting (συμπλακείς) you have got the better, but suffer him to be
amazed and to marvel at your invincible power and to say to all
that even without entering into conflict you have conquered.'''

A double crown may be won by requiting with the opposite. 60,
506, 47: "And this is the truest wonder, that we are so far from
being injured, if we are right-minded, that we are even benefited,—
and that too by the very things that we suffer unjustly at the hands
of others. Reflect then; has such an one done you an affront? You
have the power of making this affront redound to your honor. For
if you do an affront in return, you only increase the disgrace. But
if you bless him who did you the affront, you will see that all men
give you victory and proclaim your praise (ἀνακηρύττοντας). Do
you see how, by the things wherein we are wronged, we get good
done to us, if we are so minded? For if we requite with the opposite,
we are but twining a double crown about us, one for the ills which
we have suffered, as well as one for the good which we are doing."

If one can show the resignation that Job and Abraham showed, and
also cause mourning to cease, one's rewards will be numberless.
61, 390, 6: "One must have the soul of adamant who can bear with
calmness to see a child, his only one, brought up in affluence, in the
dawn of fair promise, lying upon the bier an outstretched corpse.
And if such an one, hushing to rest the heavings of nature, shall be
strengthened to say the words of Job without a tear, 'Jehovah gave,
and Jehovah hath taken away [Job I, 21],' for those words' sake
alone, he will stand with Abraham himself and with Job will be proclaimed a victor (ἀνακηρυχθήσεται). And if, staying the wailings of
the women and dissolving the bands of mourners, he shall rouse them
all to sing glory [to God], he will receive above and below rewards
unnumbered (μυρία ἄνωθεν, μυρία κάτωθεν δέξεται τὰ βραβεῖα),—
men admiring, angels applauding, God crowning him."

Abraham's victory over his nature in sacrificing Isaac is graphically portrayed in 61, 412, 24. "When he was commanded to sacrifice his son, consider how many thoughts then rose against him. Nevertheless, he brought all under submission, and all trembled before him more than before a king his guards; and with a look only he stilled them all and not one of them dared so much as mutter, but down they bowed and as to a king gave place, one and all, though much exasperated and exceeding relentless. . . . For it was the triumph in that moment of an angel, not a man. And he stood with outstretched hand, grasping not a crown, but a knife more glorious than any crown, and the throng of angels applauded and God from heaven proclaimed him conqueror (ἀνεκήρυττεν). What could be more glorious than that proclamation (κήρυγμα)? For if on occasion of a wrestler's (ἀθλητοῦ) success, not a herald below, but the king above should have risen and himself proclaimed (ἀνηγόρευσε) the Olympic victor, would not this have seemed to him more glorious than the crown and have turned the gaze of the whole theatre upon him? When then no mortal king, but God Himself, not in this theatre, but in the theatre of the universe, in the assembly of the angels, of the archangels, proclaimed his name (ἀνακηρύττη) with uplifted voice shouting from heaven, tell me what place shall we assign to this holy man?"

We should wait until the proper time for proclamation. The exposition is made fittingly on St. Matt. VI, 4: ". . . thy Father who seeth in secret shall recompense thee." 57, 275, 44: " 'Do you not wish,' says He, 'to have some as spectators of what is happening? You have not angels or archangels, but the God of all.' And if you desire to have men also as spectators, He will not deprive you of this desire at the fitting season. If you shall now make a display, you will be able to make it to ten only or twenty or (we will say) a hundred persons, but, if you take pains to lie hid now, God Himself will then proclaim (ἀνακηρύξει) you in the presence of the whole universe. Again, whereas now they who behold will rather condemn you as vainglorious, when they see you crowned so far from condemning, they will even admire you, all of them."

The athlete, after the victory is won, should not be in too great a haste to be crowned. This idea comes logically from Heb. X, 36: "For ye have need of patience, that, having done the will of God, ye may receive the promise." 63, 150, 34: "You have need of one thing only, to bear with the delay: not that you should contend (ἀθλήσητε) again. You are at the very crowns (he means); you have borne all the combats (ἀγῶνας) of bonds, of afflictions; your goods have been spoiled. What then? Henceforward you are standing to be crowned: endure this only, the delay of the crown. O the greatness of the consolation! It is as if one should speak to a wrestler (ἀθλητήν), who had overthrown (καταβαλόντα) all and had no antagonist (ἀνταγωνιστήν) and then was to be crowned and yet endured not that time, during which the president of the games (ἀγωνοθέτης) comes and places the crown upon him, and who impatiently wished to go out and escape, as though he could not bear the thirst and the heat."

There is one time of crowning for all; therefore we who are still contending should not be vexed, seeing that those who gained the victory long ago have not yet been rewarded. The comment is on Heb. XI, 37–40: ". . . they went about in sheepskins, in goatskins; being destitute, afflicted, ill-treated . . . wandering in deserts and mountains and caves and the holes of the earth. And these all received not the promise, God having provided . . . that apart from us they should not be made perfect." 63, 192, 20: "What then is their reward? They have not yet received it, but are still waiting; and after thus dying in so great tribulation they have not yet received it. They gained their victory so many ages ago and have not yet received [their reward]. And you who are yet in the conflict (ἀγῶνι), are you vexed? Do you also consider what a thing it is and how great, that Abraham and the Apostle Paul should be sitting and waiting till you have been perfected, that then they may be able to receive their reward? For the Savior has told them that, unless we also are present, He will not give it them. . . . And are you vexed that you have not yet received the reward? What then shall Abel do, who was victor before all and is sitting uncrowned? And what Noah? And what they who lived in those early times, seeing that they wait until you have been perfected and those after you? That they might not seem to have the advantage of us from being crowned before us, He appointed one time of crowning for all; and he, who gained the victory so many years before, receives his crown with you. They were before us as regards the conflicts (ἀγῶνας), but are not before us as regards the crowns."

We receive greater glory when God proclaims us, according to the remarks on St. Matt. X, 32: "Every one therefore who shall confess me before men, him will I also confess before my Father who is in heaven." 57, 402, 24: "Why hasten and hurry yourself? And why seek your rewards here, you who are 'saved by hope'? Wherefore, if you have done anything good and not received its recompense here, be not troubled (for with increase, in the time to come, the reward thereof awaits you): . . . so from the things here form your conjecture about things to come also. Why, if in the season of conflicts (ἀγώνων) they who confess are so glorious, imagine what they will be in the season of crowns. If the enemies here applaud, how shall that tenderest of fathers fail to admire and proclaim you (θαυμάσεταί σε καὶ ἀνακηρύξει)?"

Much more honor will be obtained when the Distributor of the prizes shall come. This is adduced from II Tim. II, 10: "Therefore I endure all things for the elect's sake, that they also may obtain the salvation which is in Christ Jesus with eternal glory." 62, 624, 6: "The season for being crowned is not yet come, and yet how great honor has the athlete gained! What honor then will he not obtain, when the Distributor of the prizes (ἀγωνοθέτης) shall come!"

The exhortation to be present when St. Paul and his companions are crowned is based on Phil. IV, 1: "Wherefore, my brethren beloved and longed for, my joy and crown, so stand fast in the Lord. . . ." 62, 280, 54: "Be faithful and worthy of meeting Christ, when He comes with His ineffable glory, when those meet Him, who had gone to gather the elect into the midst, when Paul and his companions, and all who in his time had been approved (εὐδοκίμησαν) are crowned, are proclaimed aloud (ἀνακηρυττομένων), are honored by the King before all His heavenly host."

We may infer from several instances how royally a winner is treated. St. Paul in his bonds is such a winner (Philemon I, 9: "yet for love's sake I rather beseech thee, being such a one as Paul the aged, and now a prisoner also of Christ Jesus"). 62, 709, 61: "For who would not receive with open arms (ὑπτίαις χερσί) an athlete who had been crowned? Who seeing him bound for Christ's sake would not have granted him ten thousand favors?"

Christ received the healed man who had been born blind as a champion, according to our author on St. John IX, 35, 38: "Jesus heard that they [the Pharisees] had cast him out; and finding him, he said, Dost thou believe on the Son of God? . . . . And he said, Lord, I believe." 59, 321, 52: "The man born blind was dishonored by those who dishonored Christ, but was honored by the Lord of angels. Such are the prizes (ἔπαθλα) of truth. . . . Therefore, like some judge in the games (ἀγωνοθέτης), He received the champion (ἀθλητήν) who had toiled much and gained the crown."

St. John Baptist was the crowned victor of the whole world even before the time of grace. 57, 188, 58: "John did not surround himself with pomp like the Greek philosophers; but he dwelt in the wilderness as in heaven, showing forth all strictness of self-restraint. And also thence, like some angel from heaven, he went down to the cities, being a champion of godliness (ἀθλητὴς εὐσεβείας) and a crowned victor (στεφανίτης) over the world and a philosopher of that philosophy which is worthy of the heavens. And these things were, when sin was not yet put away, when the law had not yet ceased, when death was not yet bound, when the brazen gates were not yet broken, but while the ancient polity was still in force. Such is the nature of a noble and thoroughly vigilant soul, for it is everywhere springing forward and passing beyond the limits (σκάμματα) set to it."

Victors are not limited to men only, but even women may surpass them in the spiritual contest. 62, 99, 10: "Men do not yield to women in wordly matters or in the games (ἄθλοις); but in the spiritual contest (πνευματικοῖς ἀγῶσι) they get the advantage over them and are the first to seize the prize (βραβεῖον)."

Women are assured of no small rewards in the comment on I Tim. II, 15: "but she [woman] shall be saved through her child-bearing, if they continue in faith and love and sanctification with sobriety." 62, 546, 3: "By these means they will have no small reward on their account, because they have trained wrestlers (ἀθλητάς) for the service of Christ."

The greatest female athlete whom St. Chrysostom mentions is, as one may naturally suppose, Olympias. He rejoices in her robust spirit and shows that more women than men are crowned victors because of their spirit and disposition. 52, 599, 28: "For not only to bear misfortunes bravely, but also to be actually insensible to them, to overlook them and with such little exertion to wreathe your brows with the garland-prize of patience, neither laboring nor toiling, neither feeling distress nor causing it to others, but as it were leaping and dancing for joy all the while,—this is indeed a proof of the most finished philosophy. Therefore I rejoice and leap for joy, I am in a flutter of delight, I am insensible to my present loneliness and the other troubles which surround me, being cheered and brightened and not a little proud on account of your greatness of soul and the repeated victories which you have won; and this not only for your own sake, but also for the sake of that large and populous city [Constantinople], where you are like a tower, a haven and a wall of defence, speaking in the eloquent voice of example and through your sufferings instructing either sex to strip readily for these contests (ἀγῶνας) and to descend into the lists (σκάμματα) with all courage and cheerfully to bear the toils which such contests (ἀγώνων ἱδρῶτας) involve. And the wonder is that without thrusting yourself into the forum or occupying the public centres of the city, but with sitting all the while in a small house and confined chamber you serve and anoint the combatants for the contest (νευροῖς, ἀλείφεις τοὺς ἑστῶτας). ... You are a chronic sufferer from the most severe infirmity, and yet more cheerfully disposed than the thriving and robust, not depressed by insults or elated by honors and glory (the latter being a cause of infinite mischief to many who, after an illustrious career in the priesthood and after reaching extreme old age and the most venerable hoar hairs, have fallen into disgrace on that account and become a common spectacle of derision for those who wish to make merry). But you on the contrary, woman as you are, clothed with a fragile body and subject to these severe attacks, have not only avoided falling into such a condition yourself, but have also prevented many others from so doing. They indeed before they had advanced far in the contest (ἀγώνων), even at the very outset and starting-point (βαλβῖδος), have been overthrown; whereas you, after having gone countless times round the farther turning-post (νύσσαν), have won a prize (βραβεῖον) in every course (δρόμον), after playing your part in manifold kinds of wrestlings and combats (παλαισμάτων καὶ ἀγώνων). And very naturally so; for the wrestlings of virtue do not depend upon age or bodily strength, but only on the spirit and the disposition. Thus women have been crowned victors, while men have been upset (ὑπεσκελίσθησαν). It is indeed always fitting to admire those who pursue virtue, but especially when some are found to cling to it at a time when many are deserting it. Therefore, my sweet lady, you deserve superlative admiration."

The crown is not only for the victor himself, but it is also shared by those who help to prepare the athlete for his contest. The preacher is an athlete of this kind whose crown may be shared by those who wait on him. This exposition is based naturally on Phil. I, 3, 5: "I thank my God upon all my remembrance of you ... for your fellowship in furtherance of the gospel from the first day until now." 62, 184, 30: "When one preaches and you wait on the preacher, you share his crowns. Since even in the games (ἀγῶσι) the crown is not only for him who strives (ἀγωνιζομένου), but also for the trainer (παιδοτρίβου), the attendant (θεραπεύοντος), and all who help to prepare (ἀσκούντων) the athlete. For they who strengthen him and recover (ἀνακτώμενοι) him may fairly participate in his victory."

How to be a partaker of the crown is mentioned in the case of Onesiphorus, II Tim. I, 18: "(the Lord grant unto him to find mercy of the Lord in that day); and in how many things he ministered at Ephesus, thou knowest very well." 62, 614, 26: "The faithful not only benefit those in danger, but even make themselves partakers of the crowns due to them. There may be one of those who are devoted to God, who is visited with affliction and is maintaining the conflict (ἀθλῶν) with great fortitude, while you are not yet dragged to this conflict (ἀγῶνα). It is in your power without entering into the course (στάδιον) to be a sharer of the crowns reserved for him, by standing by him, preparing his mind (ἀλείφοντι), animating and exciting him (διεγείροντι). . . . He, who relieves the combatant (ἀθλητῇ) when wasted with hunger, who stands by him, encouraging him by words and rendering him every service, is not inferior to the combatant (ἀθλοῦντι). For do not suppose that Paul the combatant (ἀθλητήν), that irresistible and invincible one (ἀκαταγώνιστον), but some one of the many, who, if he had not received much consolation and encouragement, would not perhaps have stood, would not have contended (ἠγωνίσατο). So those who are out of the contest (ἀγώνων) may perchance be the cause of victory to him who is engaged in it and may be partakers of the crowns reserved for the victor."

Occasion is also taken to comment on Col. IV, 11: ". . . these only are my fellow-workers unto the kingdom of God, men that have been a comfort unto me." 62, 377, 54: "When we comfort the Saints by presence, by words, by assiduous attendance, when we suffer adversity together with them 'that are in bonds,' he says, 'as bound with them [Heb. XIII, 3],' when we make their sufferings ours, we shall also be partakers in their crowns. Have you not been dragged to the stadium? Have you not entered into the contest (ἀγῶνα)? It is another who strips himself, another who wrestles (παλαίει); but if you are so minded, you too shall be a sharer. Anoint him, become his favorer and partisan (φιλητής καὶ σπουδαστής), from without the lists shout (ἐπιβόα) loudly for him, stir up (διέγειρε) his strength, refresh (ἀνακτῶ) his spirit."

We become partakers of the prizes of others by almsgiving, particularly if it is done cheerfully. 62, 188, 13: " 'God loveth a cheerful giver [II Cor. IX, 7].' If one does not so give, let him not give: for that is loss, not alms. If then you know that you will gain, not they, know that your gain becomes greater. For as for them the body is fed, but your soul is approved. Let us share in their contests (ἄθλων), that we may share also in their great prizes (ἐπάθλων)."

The matter of rejoicing and envying in the case of those who win the crown is clearly demonstrated in 62, 378, 34. "See you not in the case of the athletes, how the one is crowned, the other is not crowned; but the grief and the joy is among the favorers (ἐραστῶν) and disfavorers (μισούντων), these are they who leap (πηδῶσιν), they who caper (σκιρτῶσιν)? See how great a thing is not envying. Another wears the crown, and you leap, you are gay. But they also know well that what has been done is common. Therefore the envious do not accuse the partisan of the victor indeed, but they try to beat down the victory; and you hear them saying such words as these, '[There] I expunged you (ἐξήλειψά σε)' and 'I beat you down (κατέβαλόν σε).'"

In 59, 212, 4 we share in the crown by rejoicing with him who labors. "Let us consider this, that, as we offend God when we waste with envy at other men's blessings, so when we rejoice with them we are well pleasing to Him and make ourselves partakers of the good things reserved for the righteous. Therefore Paul exhorts us to 'rejoice with them that rejoice [Rom. XII, 15]'.... Considering then that, even when we labor not, by rejoicing with him who labors, we become sharers of his crown, let us cast aside all envy and implant charity in our souls, that, by applauding those of our brethren who are well pleasing to God, we may obtain both present and future good things."

There is a triple crown for the person who casts down envy and rejoices in the success of another, as St. Chrysostom explains in interpreting Col. IV, 11: "...these only are my fellow-workers unto the kingdom of God, men that have been a comfort unto me." 62, 379, 21: "You ought rather to be crowned than he, as your contest (ἀγών) is the more brilliant. One crown which you win is against envy; another is the one with which you are encircled by love. For the sharing in his joy is a proof not only of your being free from envy, but also of being rooted in love. The third crown consists in this, that, whereas men below applaud the one who is victorious, the angels above applaud you; also this man is crowned openly, but you are crowned in secret, where your Father sees."

It seems quite natural that St. Paul, the greatest human athlete of all the splendid galaxy which Holy Writ presents to view, should stand preëminent in our thought as we close this study of the Christian Athlete whom St. Chrysostom has so graphically and sympathetically portrayed. The last point made is that, although the rewards are greater than the contest, yet the athlete must not be so elated as to cease from greater efforts. The comment is on Rom. VIII, 18: "... the sufferings of this present time are not worthy to be compared with the glory which shall be revealed to us-ward." 60, 528, 59: "Observe how he [St. Paul] at once allays and rouses the spirit of the combatants (ἀγωνιζομένων). For after he had shown that the rewards (ἔπαθλα) were greater than the labors, he both exhorts to greater efforts and yet will not let them be elated, as being still outdone by the crowns given in requital."

St. Paul himself is not content with overcoming once, but he contends anew in order to enhance the splendor of the victory. The reference is to I Cor. II, 2: "For I determined not to know anything among you, save Jesus Christ, and him crucified." 61, 47, 32: "Nothing was ever more prepared for combat (ἀγωνιστικώτερον) than the spirit of Paul; or, rather, nothing was ever equal to the grace working within him, which overcomes all things. For what had been previously said is sufficient indeed to cast down the pride of the boasters about wisdom; nay, even a part of it had been enough. But to enhance the splendor of the victory he contends anew (ἐπαγωνίζεται) for the points which he had affirmed."

Tempting and alluring as the crown may be, yet the Christian Athlete may well take the attitude of St. Paul, who preferred to keep on contending instead of stopping to receive the prize. Phil. I, 23–25: "... having the desire to depart and be with Christ; ... yet ... I know that I shall abide, yea, and abide with you all, for your progress and joy in the faith." 62, 206, 3: "What wrestler (ἀγωνιστής), when he could be crowned, would prefer to contend (ἀγωνίζεσθαι)? What boxer (πυκτεύων), when he could be wreathed with the crown, would choose to enter afresh into the contest (ἀγῶνα) and offer his head to wounds (κατακόπτειν)? .... O that spirit of Paul! Nothing was ever like it, nor ever will be!"

CONCLUSION

After reading the Biblical Homilies of St. Chrysostom for the purpose of noting all allusions to athletics, one cannot fail to be impressed with the spell that the Greek Olympic games must have still exercised in the days of St. Chrysostom when he addressed his congregations both in Antioch and in Constantinople. Athletics must have had a strong appeal to the people, else St. Chrysostom would not have resorted to them so often for illustration. Since the major part of his life was spent in Antioch and since most of his Homilies were delivered there, we may fairly assume that whenever he used athletic terms, he had in mind the games which were held in Antioch, at that time the fourth city in importance in the Roman Empire.[1]

The frequency of St. Chrysostom's use of athletic metaphors is also most apparent to the reader, when comparison is made with the use of other types of metaphors such as those pertaining to the sea, agriculture, building, etc. It is true that military metaphors are quite abundant, but this must be expected since soldiers were everywhere very common and wars were by no means unknown. As a matter of statistics it would not be an unprofitable undertaking to tabulate the use of metaphors of all kinds in St. Chrysostom's works, which would enable one to see the exact ratio of athletic metaphors to all the others.

However, the general impression which the reader gains as he turns the pages of St. Chrysostom is that athletics held as strong a fascination for the average person of that day as they do at the present. The zeal, interest and attention that a distinguished wrestler arouses, such as is depicted in the beginning of the chapter on Wrestling, finds its modern parallel in the interest shown in any wrestling- or boxing-contest of major importance.

---

[1]Founded by Antiochus Epiphanes (175–164), the games in Antioch were held in the suburb of Daphne and were given the title of Olympia by the Eleans in 44 A. D. Their interest lies in the fact that the model of Olympia was followed in every particular, not only in the programme and administration, but also in the relations existing between Daphne and Antioch, which corresponded entirely to those between Olympia and Elis. In the fourth century a fierce dispute arose between the popular party, which wished to transfer the important part of the festival from Daphne to Antioch, and the conservative party headed by Libanius, who characterized the proposed change as sacrilege and a violation of the true Olympia. The games continued to be celebrated as late as the reign of Justinus in the sixth century.

A comparison of the length of the several chapters reveals the fact that wrestling ranks as the contest *par excellence*. The foot-race takes second place in interest (judging from the decided superiority accorded to it over boxing), while chariot-racing ranks a low fourth. The ratio of running to wrestling is somewhat higher than that of boxing to running.

This study of St. Chrysostom is most valuable for its vivid and graphic portrayal of the life of the people of Antioch and Constantinople in the latter part of the fourth century, revealing the extremely human nature of both the athletes themselves and those who were their spectators. Under the glowing descriptions of St. Chrysostom they live for us in a way which we can sympathetically understand. Many technical points of interest regarding the games and the regulations prescribed for their conduct and that of the athletes themselves have been unconsciously revealed to us by St. Chrysostom from time to time. Finally, it may be suggested that many Biblical characters live anew for us in the athletic *rôle* with which St. Chrysostom has invested them.

INDEX OF ATHLETIC TERMS

ἀγαπητός 51

ἀγών 11, 12 (2), 13, 14, 15 (2), 16, 18 (3), 19 (3), 20 (2), 21 (3), 22 (2), 25 (3), 26 (2), 29, 30, 31 (2), 33 (3), 34 (2), 39, 43 (2), 44 (2), 45, 46 (5), 48, 49 (2), 50 (2), 51, 54, 55 (3), 56, 59 (3), 60, 61, 66 (3), 67 (4), 68 (2), 70 (2), 78, 79 (2), 80 (3), 81 (2), 82 (3), 83 (4), 84 (2), 85 (3), 86, 87 (2), 88 (4), 89, 90, 91, 92, 93, 95 (4), 96 (2), 97 (3), 98 (3), 99 (2), 103 (3), 104, 105, 106 (5), 107 (3), 108, 109

ἀγωνία 55, 83

ἀγωνίζεσθαι 11, 15, 19, 22, 24, 30, 31 (3), 37 (2), 38, 44, 45, 46 (2), 49, 51, 52, 53 (2), 56, 59, 61, 68, 71 (2), 74, 78, 80, 81, 82, 83 (3), 85, 86 (4), 87, 88 (2), 89, 93, 94 (4), 96, 99 (2), 106, 107, 109 (2)

ἀγώνισμα 16, 29, 52, 56, 94

ἀγωνιστής 53, 71, 80, 109

ἀγωνιστικώτερος 109

ἀγωνοθετεῖν 50, 76

ἀγωνοθέτης 19, 31, 32 (2), 33 (2), 34, 46, 50, 57, 75, 76, 80, 85, 90, 94, 103, 104 (2)

ἀδόκμιος 15, 29

ἀήρ 69, 72

ἀθλεῖν 23, 30, 51, 66, 69, 83, 86, 90, 92 (2), 102, 107 (2)

ἄθλησις 10, 15 (2), 33, 52 (2), 67, 84

ἀθλητής 12 (2), 14, 15, 17, 20, 21, 23, 25 (3), 30, 34, 47, 50, 52 (2), 53, 54, 55 (3), 57, 58 (2), 59, 62, 64 (4), 67, 85, 89, 98, 102, 103, 104, 105 (2), 107 (2)

ἄθλος 20, 39, 41, 53, 58, 62, 70, 78, 87, 89, 105, 108

ἀθλοφόρος 32

ἀκαταγώνιστος 14, 83, 107

ἀκμάζειν 85

ἀκονιτί 47

ἀκρίβεια 12, 84

ἀλείφειν 11, 13, 22, 23 (3), 24 (2), 25, 26 (2), 27, 41, 57 (2), 93, 106, 107

ἅμιλλα 77

ἀναγορεύειν 102

ἀναδέχεσθαι 35

ἀνακήρυξις 23, 90, 99

ἀνακηρύσσειν 26, 34, 35, 62, 87, 91, 93, 98, 99, 101 (3), 102 (3), 104 (2)

ἀνακτᾶσθαι 23, 52, 71, 107 (2)

ἀνάλωτος 57

ἀναπαλαίειν 54

ἀνάπαυσις 87

ἀναπνεῖν 24, 25, 67

ἀναστρέφειν 84

ἄνεσις 81

ἀνήρ 55

ἀνιστάναι 68

ἀνταγωνίζεσθαι 86

ἀνταγωνιστής 14, 20, 21, 31, 49, 66, 70, 79, 100, 103

ἀνταίρειν 66 (2)

ἀντίπαλος 13, 17, 50, 51, 61, 71 (2), 85

ἀπιέναι 35

ἀπείραστος 29

ἀποδύειν 60

ἀποκρούειν 70

ἀπολείπειν 35

ἅπτειν 25, 53

ἁρπάζειν 43

ἀσκεῖν 43, 107

ἄσκησις 10, 15, 19, 29

αὐχμός 52

ἀχείρωτος 57

βαλβίς 68, 84, 106

βραβεῖον 13, 16, 19, 31, 32, 33 (2), 37, 41 (3), 43 (4), 44 (2), 49, 51, 66, 69, 75, 76, 82, 84 (2), 86, 87, 92, 93 (2), 94, 95, 96 (2), 97 (2), 98, 99 (3), 100 (2), 101, 105, 106

114

βραβεύειν 32, 33, 56 (2), 86, 98
βραβευτής 33

γαστρίζειν 74
γαστριμαργία 30
γενναῖος 24, 47, 55, 56, 62, 64,
  67, 68
γενναίως 68
γρυπός 30
γυμνάζειν 11 (4), 14 (4), 15, 18
  (3), 19, 21 (3), 22, 23, 24, 25
  (2), 34, 66, 87
γυμνασία 10, 14 (2), 18, 19 (2),
  25, 50, 55
γυμνάσιον 10, 12 (4), 13, 14, 16,
  18, 21 (2), 25, 30

δάκνειν 93
δέρειν ἀέρα 72
διάβροχος 67
δίαιτα 31
διακόπτειν 40 (2)
διαλύειν 16, 37
διαμαρτάνειν 37
διανιστάναι 44
διανύειν 44
διατρέχειν 15, 77
δίαυλος 35 (2), 38, 40, 42, 44, 48
διαχεῖν 98
διδάσκαλος 16
διδόναι λαβάς 61
διεγείρειν 23, 44, 107 (2)
διολισθαίνειν 57
διωγμός 69
διώκειν 41
δοκιμασία 30
δόκιμος 22 (2)
δόλιχος 35
δριμύς 94
δρομεύς 42, 45
δρόμος 10, 15, 35 (2), 36 (2),
  37 (3), 38, 39, 40 (2), 41, 42,
  43 (2), 45 (2), 46, 76, 79, 106
δύναμις 30, 69
δυσκαταγώνιστος 60
δυσκίνητος 51

ἐγγυμνάζειν 11, 14, 18, 22, 26 (2)
ἐγείρειν 44
ἐγκρατεύεσθαι 30
ἐκλύειν 30, 45
ἐκπηδᾶν 86
ἐκτείνειν 20
ἐκτενῶς 41 (2)
ἔλαιον 11, 57, 67
ἕλκειν 88, 97 (2)
ἐναγώνιος 19, 23, 24, 41, 67,
  82 (3), 94
ἐνεργεῖν 66 (2)
ἐνιζάνειν 57
ἐξαλείφειν 108
ἐξασκεῖν 10
ἐξέρχεσθαι 46
ἐξουσία 50
ἐπάγειν 71
ἐπαγωνίζεσθαι 109
ἔπαθλον 14, 30, 42, 49, 72, 82 (2),
  90, 91, 92 (2), 93 (3), 94 (4),
  95 (3), 96 (2), 97 (2), 98, 100,
  104, 108, 109
ἐπαίρειν 71
ἐπεκτείνειν 41
ἐπηρεάζειν 20, 33
ἐπήρεια 32
ἐπιβοᾶν 107
ἐπιλαμβάνειν 41
ἐπιπηδᾶν 39, 88
ἐπιστήμη 12
ἐπιστήμων 30
ἐπιτείνειν 43
ἐπιτήδειος 22
ἐπιτυγχάνειν 19, 39
ἐραστής 108
εὐδοκιμεῖν 104
εὐεξία 66
εὐκαταγώνιστος 79
εὐρυχωρία 70
εὐσέβεια 11, 105
εὐτρεπής 16
εὐφημία 76
εὐχερής 79

ἡνίοχος 18, 51, 73, 74

θαυμάζειν 26, 104
θαυμαστής 31
θέατρον 52 (2), 54, 56
θεραπεία 31
θεραπεύειν 106
θύλακος 15, 21

ἱδρώς 35, 106
ἱμάτιον 67
ἱπποδρομία 75, 94
ἵππος 77
ἱπποτρόφος 32
ἱστάναι 17, 68, 106
ἰσχνότερος 50
ἰσχυρός 30
ἰσχυρότερος 50
ἰσχύς 47

καίριος 70, 71 (4)
καταβάλλειν 51, 62, 66, 103, 108
καταβραβεύειν 33 (3)
καταγωνίζεσθαι 12
κατακόπτειν 69 (2), 109
καταλαμβάνειν 35
κατάνεσθαι 87
καταπαλαίειν 13, 52, 60
καταπίπτειν 53
κενοῦν 69
κήρυγμα 102
κολοφών 62, 70
κονίειν 55 (2)
κόπτειν 66
κότινος 46
κροτεύειν 93

λαβή 16, 17, 19, 40, 48, 57 (2), 61, 62
λαμπρός 21, 48
λαμπρότερος 91
λιπαίνειν 71

μαθητής 17
μακρὸς ὁ δίαυλος 35, 48
μακρότερος ὁ δίαυλος 38
μέλας 55
μετριάζειν 24
μισεῖν 108

νευροῦν 106
νικᾶν 33, 79
νόμος 15, 31 (2), 57
νοσεῖν 13
νύσσα 77, 106

Ὀλυμπιονίκης 90

παγκρατιάζειν 69
παγκρατιαστής 65, 68
παγκράτιον 15, 96
παιδοτριβεῖν 13
παιδοτρίβης 10, 15 (2), 16 (2), 17 (2), 20, 21, 24'(2), 85, 106
πάλαισμα 18, 19, 33, 48 (2), 49 (2), 50, 57, 58, 60, 61 (2), 79, 95, 97, 98, 100, 106
παλαιστής 17
παλαίστρα 11 (3), 12 (4), 15, 17 (2), 19, 20 (2), 21, 25
παλαίειν 17, 35, 56, 60, 62, 89, 100, 107
πάλη 11, 20, 51 (2), 52, 54, 57 (2), 59, 61, 96, 97
πατάσσειν 66
πένταθλος 21
περιτρέπειν 63, 66, 68, 71
πηδᾶν 78 (2), 108
πληγή 68 (2), 70 (2), 71 (4), 94
πλήσσειν 67
πνευματικός 105
προθυμία 26
προλαμβάνειν 76 (2)
προπηδᾶν 84
προσπαλαίειν 33
πτῶμα 19, 53
πυκτεύειν 17 (2), 19, 26, 35, 65, 66, 67 (4), 68 (2), 69 (2), 71 (2), 89, 94, 95, 96, 99, 109
πύκτης 14, 67, 69, 71

ῥᾳθυμεῖν 19, 61
ῥᾳθυμότερος 56
ῥᾳστώνη 53

σιμός 30
σιτίον 15

σκάμμα 13, 20 (3), 37 (2), 48 (2), 50, 52, 53, 54, 58, 63, 64, 67, 78 (2), 82 (2), 84 (2), 86, 89, 105, 106
σκιαμαχεῖν 72
σκιαμαχία 71, 72
σκιρτᾶν 108
σκίρτημα 75
σοφός 24
σπουδάζειν 19
σπουδαστής 31, 107
στάδιον 11, 19, 23, 33, 36, 40, 41, 44, 45, 46, 51, 52, 55, 66, 68, 77, 82, 93, 94, 99, 107
στεφανίτης 47, 64, 66, 105
στέφανος 19, 23, 78, 79, 82, 91
στεφανοῦν 89
συγκροτεῖν 13
σύμμετρος 79
συμπλέκειν 15, 17 (2), 47, 60, 61, 100, 101 (2)
συμπλοκή 57, 66, 100, 101
συναγωνίζεσθαι 85

συνεφάπτεσθαι 39 (2), 59
σῶμα 17
σωματικός 30

τελεῖν 46
τέχνη 47, 48
τραῦμα 66
τρέχειν 38, 39 (2), 44, 74, 89
τρίζειν 50
τυγχάνειν 78

ὑπερβαίνειν 76, 85
ὑπόθεσις 95
ὑποσκελίζειν 57, 58, 106
ὕπτιος 104
ὑπωπιάζειν 15
ὑστερεῖν 26, 36, 40, 76
ὕστερος 44

φιλητής 107
φιλοσοφεῖν 38, 56, 99
φιλοσοφία 12 (2)

χείρ 66